Black, Queer and Blessed

Black, Queer and Blessed

My Story and the Biblical Story
Churches Don't Teach

Rev. A. Leon Tredwell, PhD.

Exodus Literature LLC

This volume is dedicated to "Bernie Boo and Leon Charles," for giving gifts that can never be taken away.

Table of Contents

Praise for Black, Queer and Blessed

"In drawing an analogous relationship between the prophetic and political tensions between Jeremiah and Hananiah of the Hebrew Bible and Martin Luther King, Jr. and Malcolm X of the 20th century Black Radical Tradition, Tredwell invites readers to abandon the myth of objectivity in biblical and theological hermeneutics. By situating Ebed-Melech, the Cushite eunuch of King Zedekiah's court, as a third exemplar of prophetic intervention to consider, *Black, Queer and Blessed* invites readers to embrace the reality that those deemed foreign and queer within our communities are crucial to the work of bending the arc of the moral universe towards divine justice."

Michele E. Watkins, Ph.D.

Assistant Professor of Theology and Religious Studies,

St. John's University, Jamaica, New York

Immediate Past Executive Director, Society for the Study of Black Religion

NEH Faculty Fellow, Orthodox Christian Studies Center at Fordham University

"My, my. *Black, Queer and Blessed* is the balm of healing Rev. Dr. Tredwell intends it to be. With the cadence of a preacher, the artistry of a musician, the mentorship of a teacher, and the precision of a scholar, Rev. Dr. Tredwell takes us on a captivating journey of celebrating Queer Black Excellence. Building upon his lived experience and biblical scholarship, *Black, Queer and Blessed* is full of revelations and insights that leave even the most well-versed biblical student...turning its pages with eager anticipation. You will not view Scripture/Word of God, or the Resurrection the same ever again. This book is for biblical scholars, preachers, pastors, Sunday School teachers, and everyday people who yearn to see a deeper connection between the pages of the Scripture and their own lives."

Reverend Anne J. Scalfaro

Senior Pastor

Calvary Baptist Church of Denver

"*Black, Queer and Blessed*, a poignant exploration of identity that powerfully captures the intersection of race, sexuality, and spirituality. Weaving together personal stories, cultural insights, and deeply resonant reflections, it serves not only as a testament to the beauty and complexity of Black queer lives, but also as a call for understanding, acceptance, and community. With its evocative prose and heartfelt authenticity, *Black, Queer and Blessed* stands out as an essential contribution to contemporary literature and social discourse. I wholeheartedly recommend this book to anyone seeking to broaden their understanding of the diverse human experience and celebrate the historically marginalized voices."

Reverend Benjamin Ledell Bragg-Reynolds

Pastor

Peoples Congregational United Church of Christ, Washington, DC

"I've known Dr. Lee, the author of *Black, Queer and Blessed*, for over 30 years. For much of that time, I celebrated his gifts, witnessed his brilliance, and admired the grace with which he carried himself, without ever truly knowing the depth of the pain he bore in silence. This book was not just a reading experience for me; it was a revelation. It opened a door into the quiet war he waged with identity, faith, and belonging—all while navigating the complexities of being Black, Queer, and faithful in the context of the Black Church.

This work is both memoir and theological reflection, but at its core, it is an unfiltered account of one man's fight to live fully and truthfully in the tension between who he is and the institution that shaped him. What struck me most was the courage to confront long-standing norms—not with bitterness, but with deep yearning for reconciliation and healing.

The book doesn't ask for agreement. In fact, it challenged me on many levels, especially in areas where my theology and convictions differ. But what it does ask—what it demands—is to be heard. To be seen. To be considered. It invites us into a world where silence has often been mistaken for peace, and where applause has often masked agony.

Through raw storytelling, biblical reflection, and cultural critique, *Black, Queer and Blessed* offers an urgent and tender challenge to the Black Church. It doesn't tear down—it calls forth. It asks us, especially those who claim to love and lead, whether we're truly willing to hold space for the wounded, the different, the unseen.

This book blessed me. It broke my heart. And it left me with a renewed commitment to listen more deeply—especially to those whose pain has been buried beneath our praise."

Dr. Stephen Crawford

President and Founder

Experience Leadership, Minneapolis, Minnesota

"Dr. Tredwell takes the reader on a journey, both personal and theological, as he seeks to come to terms with the fullness of who he is as a Queer Black man in a world that despises and rejects both.

Every person who has lived with the existential reality of rejection and humiliation has sought to find some kind of acceptance with and in the Creator, and more than in a general sense, but in the particular.

They have asked, not unlike the author, particularly if they are Christian, 'Is there anyone in the sacred pages of scripture who looks like me? Is there anyone who looks like me that God affirms?'

Dr. Tredwell finds that person in Ebed-Melech, a Queer, castrated man who finds favor with a King and with God.

This is a book for our times where the issue of sexuality has been both politicized and weaponized.

It is a must read for every judicatory head, for every Pastor and for every person who is seeking to find acceptance to all of who they are including their Queerness.

Nothing that God creates is unclean."

Reverend Kenneth W. Wheeler
Retired Clergy
Evangelical Lutheran Church in America

Foreword

In an era when the Bible, for many, has become little more than scrollable text hidden inside a smartphone app, Rev. Dr. Arthur Lee Tredwell delivers an urgently needed reminder that—as the writer of Hebrews claimed—the "Word of God truly is alive, active, and sharper than any two-edged sword."

In this beautifully composed and honestly rendered book, Tredwell juxtaposes two compelling narratives. First, he offers his own tale of becoming, leading us through the rich and robust story of a young Black man finding his way in a complex, often contradictory world of race, religion, and relationships. These experiences qualify him to speak with authority as a same-gender-loving pastor and preacher of color who has navigated both sides of many coins. Throughout, I found myself pausing to envision the prose pictures he paints so beautifully, taking moments to hear the music of joy and the groans of struggle that accompany his progress. The path is not always clear. But over time, it is increasingly obvious a remarkable presence and voice are emerging in the person of this divinely called and well-equipped pastor.

Then, to our delight, Tredwell takes us right into his preacher heart, as he interprets the biblical account of Ebed-Melech, the eunuch who rescues the prophet Jeremiah from his imprisonment at the hands of corrupt power. Employing the time-tested approach of "rereading" the text—as the late great Delores Williams called it—Tredwell compels us to pay close attention to the words, historical context, and finally his (and our own) lived experience as a person in the margins, searching the scripture for light and guidance in our quests for self-acceptance, healing, and wholeness.

This is a wonderful book. It speaks to anyone who has been minimized or rejected as "unfit" and "unworthy" to do sacred work at a time when so many are taking advantage of unholy opportunities to oppress, divide, and destroy. But I would argue this book is particularly powerful for queer people of color and same-gender-loving individuals who need to find and relish their own reflections in the sacred texts. Tredwell's ability to blend scholarly weight and queer sensibilities (especially those found in Black church vernacular) makes Black, Queer, and Blessed a joy to read. Moreover, it compels anyone who may (mistakenly) believe they have no place in God's kingdom to come right in and take their already-reserved seat at the table.

The reason so many purveyors of exclusionary gospels and homophobic dogmas skim over the story of Ebed-Melech the faithful eunuch is obvious enough. But it's equally obvious why we need this book. Both stories—Tredwell's and Ebed-Melech's—are gifts we should treasure. They bear telling because they bear witness to an essential eternal truth: no one and nothing is hidden from God's eyes. We are all seen exactly as we are, fit for service, and called to faithfulness. This book is a blessing!

Bishop Tim Wolfe
Midwest Region, The Fellowship of Affirming Ministries

Preface

Black, Queer and Blessed is the result of the confluence of two prolonged musings. The first surfaced as I was completing my Masters of Religion and Theology at United Theological Seminary in St. Paul, Minnesota. I was inspired by the significant parallels between the Hananiah/Jeremiah debate in Jeremiah 28, and the political philosophies of Malcolm X and Dr. Martin Luther King, Jr. Hananiah, a true nationalist, prophesied in opposition to Jeremiah that the destruction of Judah would not occur. He believed that all of the wealth that Nebuchadnezzar had already taken would be restored within a two-year period. Jeremiah conversely had been prophesying the destruction of Judah and advising the people to integrate and assimilate into Babylonian society. In chapter 29: 5-7, Jeremiah prophecies these words from Yahweh:

> *Build houses and dwell in them; plant gardens and eat their*
> *fruit Take wives and beget sons and daughters; and take wives for*
> *your sons and give your daughters to husbands, so that they may*
> *bear sons and daughters—that you may be increased there, and*

not diminished. And seek the peace of the city where I have caused you to be carried away captive, and pray to the Lord for it; for in its peace, you will have peace.

However, after this discovery, I had a "nagging" sense that the book of Jeremiah held some additional Word that would resonate even closer to my heart.

Toward the middle of my Doctoral studies, I came across the Ebed-Melech narrative; a story of direct interface between Yahweh and a Black Queer man – in fact, a transgender man. A story where Yahweh calls the Black Queer man, then plots, plans and executes the rescue of Yahweh's prophet Jeremiah, who had been thrown into a cistern to die.

The second musing emerged around this time and was a question as to the source of theological reflection. Can sound theology only emerge from the study of the classical theologians, many of whom did not fully recognize Black humanity? Or, are their other viable sources? And, more importantly, is the lived experience of Black and Queer Americans a viable source of theology? I conclude that it is.

To that end, this book is written as a "balm," to bring healing, inspiration, and biblical correction to every Black Queer individual who has been traumatized by churches that preach and teach the six "clobber passages." It is written to every young/old person, regardless of ethnicity, who identifies as Queer. It is written to every parent of a child who discovers their unique sexuality and gender expression. It is written to Black preachers, particularly those who are without formal theological training, as a corrective as to where Yahweh stands on the matter of Queerness. It is written as support for the United Methodist Church and similar denominations who have openly and painfully wrestled with this issue.

I want to acknowledge the contributions of professors, family, and friends who stood by me during the elongated process of bringing this project to completion. Particular thanks to Dr. Vincent Harding, Dr. Carolyn Pressler, the late Dr. R. Weiss, and Dr. Arthur Jones for your encouragement. Special thanks to my granddaughter, Naja, for her beautiful illustration of "wrestling with God" that separates the book sections. And to my editor, Misti Aas, who also exhibited great patience and faith in the process.

May this book bless each reader in the profound manner in which it has inspired me.

-Dr. Lee

I.

Witness

Prelude

There's a man over the river, giving sight to the blind.
—Traditional

All of us who love Black Churches approach our critiques with great trepidation. How dare we critique the Black Church? From hush harbors during enslavement to modern cathedrals, Black Churches have pressed their way forward, evolving to heights of institutionalism in a context that deems Black life disposable, so that white life may be enriched.

As we enter the 400th year of Black life on these shores, Black Churches are continually forced to wrestle with the tensions arising from the richness of their life-giving contributions, while navigating the ever-evolving post-colonial American context in which they reside. It is not their physical manifestations we call into question, but rather their constructs of leadership, development, spirituality, and processes of preaching relevant theology that scream out, "Critique!" Consider the following paradigm:

Long-standing mentor the Reverend Dr. Willa Grant Battle, founding pastor of the then House of Refuge, now Grace Temple Deliverance Center of Minneapolis, Minnesota, describes a familiar scene of transition for African Americans in the rural South in the first quarter of the 20th century. She recounts, when a family was fortunate enough, or necessity demanded a move from one house to another, most families utilized a well-known process and strategy.

Having packed all their belongings, the family wagon would be brought around to the front of the house and placed as evenly as possible with the front porch and front door, in order to facilitate the easiest loading process. Then, all the family's possessions, box by box, piece by piece, would be loaded into the wagon. Once this process was completed, the family mule, or mules, would be brought around to the front of the house and hitched to the front of the wagon.

With the mule securely in place, the last activity to be completed before the family boarded the wagon was to round up the dogs. One by one, the dogs would be securely tied to the very back of the wagon. With this task accomplished, family members would board the wagon and the male or female head of the household would take the reins, steering the mule to the road and heading in the direction of the family's new dwelling.

Somewhere between the three-quarters and one mile mark, a certain instinctual clarity would strike the consciousness of the dogs, alerting them to the full understanding that the family was moving - leaving the homestead, heading to parts unknown to them. When this recognition sunk in, the dogs would immediately take on a different demeanor. In concert, they would begin to bark and growl, alerting each other to their shared inextricable, impending apocalypse.

As the alarm became reality to the full canine cohort, communal resistance would break out. Some dogs would attempt to turn their backs to the wagon, digging in their claws with eyes bulging, saliva dripping, straining their muscles with all their might to stop the wagon. The source of their distress? The theory being buried bones in the yard; bones they were being forced to leave, bones they would never be able to retrieve again.

8

Despite their arduous efforts of resistance, the dogs were no competition for the power of the mule. The mule, wearing blinders, never saw the dogs, and may only have heard their growls in the distance; dismissing them, continuing to function as programmed, pulling the family's possessions down the dusty road.

Dr. Battle, a dominating matriarch who earned her doctorate in mid-life, would often tell this story during periods of discontent and disagreement within the congregation, positioning her opponents as "those concerned about bones," and her leadership as the "driving force" taking the church family to a better place. She was then, and is now at 100 years of age, an inspired leader and pastoral genius. Often, after telling the story, she would lead the congregation into a period of sustained prayer that our hearts and minds might meld into one accord. It is in that same spirit of unity that I now offer this prayer for Black Churches for self-knowledge, discernment, agency, creativity, liminality, and power tempered by compassion.

1

I wouldn't have religion.... I couldn't feel sometime.
—Traditional

The white, gold-trimmed casket resting above the open grave gradually resolved into a sight of astonishment as the rite of burial unfolded. As the coffin lid was raised for the final glimpse, it immediately blocked the fullness of the sinking autumn sun. Yet, almost seamlessly, those rays and their warmth surrounded the entire bier, providing a celestial backdrop of golden yellow. This momentary still-life was so poignant, that even in my grief, I chuckled marveling, 'An elegant, grand Black lady to the very end.'

Really, who does that? Who summons the sun to highlight their last earthly viewing in declaration and celebration of their entrance into the eternal? Momma – Bernie Boo!

She was arrayed as requested in a style of Southern Black Baptist elegance. The Women's Missionary Society of our church, Mt. Olive Baptist, had given her a button- down, pink and white trimmed floral house coat. The type of dress that a refined lady might wear in sickness when she is receiving guests. Momma never wore it, but saved it for her shroud. The house coat was complimented with a white pearl necklace and earrings, accompanied by white gloves.

Momma, a practicing beautician most of her life, lost her hair to chemo, but had also put aside a new, shorter-cut, dark brown wig. She had prearranged with our family friend, Ms. Alene, to do her makeup. The chemo had caused dark spots on her cheeks, adding puffiness in her face and particularly her jaws, so her face was fuller than normal. The darker skin discoloration, a byproduct of the toxic therapy, was a visible scar of her battle with cancer. Yet, with all factors considered, she looked peaceful.

Most of the family was present. My mother's siblings, Aunt Alease and Aunt Mary, and their brother, Uncle Henderson. My father's sisters were also present; Aunt Louise, whom we called "Pooh," my Aunt Lucy, and my Aunt Blanche. Aunt Blanche was my and Momma's favorite.

But, on this day of her Homegoing we were seated as the immediate family and Momma's next of kin. To my left was Daddy, subtly smelling of a mixture of gin and Old Spice, traumatized by the implications of his loss, weeping bitterly. To my right was my costly Caucasian wife of five years, displaying minimal emotion and beautifully striking in a deep navy-colored dress we had just acquired for the occasion. Her auburn hair glistened from the setting sun.

I wept alongside my father, but had I fully recognized the impending implications of my loss, I would have cried more bitterly.

Fourteen days earlier, I had flown from Minneapolis to Norfolk, Virginia to see Momma and Daddy. All the signs of her imminent transition were demonstrable, and yet I reasoned beyond them. In my mind, people didn't suddenly die of cancer. Cancer was a progressive, degenerative disease. People went into the hospital and lingered for months until they died. That was not what I was seeing on this visit. Momma was not in the hospital and she was mobile. Not running track, but mobile. Sure, she was cautious in how she used her energy - like on that Saturday when we went to buy new furniture for the den.

I pulled up to the furniture store. Daddy was in the back seat and Momma was in the passenger seat up-front with me. When I opened the door for her to get out, she swung her legs around and I gently helped her up and out of the car.

When we got inside, she said to me, "Now, this is how we are going to do this... I'm going to sit here in the front of the store. You and your daddy will pick out the pieces of furniture that you like. Once you guys have made that decision, come back and get me and I will come see your choices and give the final approval."

We did just that. She walked a little slow, but so what?

Having approved of our selections, we headed to the car. Once seated, sideways in the front passenger seat, she asked me to lift her legs as she twisted forward. I just thought it was a ploy for a little more attention from her only child, and I shrugged it off.

That evening after dinner, Momma called me to the back room - my former bedroom. She had opened the family safe. She took out several papers; her birth certificate, their marriage license, the deed on the house - showing me all the family's important documentation. I interpreted this as simply letting me know where to look for documents...when the time came. Which in my mind was still several months away. I felt honored by the disclosure and saw it as a kind of rite of passage. It felt as if she was saying that at her transition I would be head of the family. My father's alcoholism had long ago prevented him from handling any major business matters.

■ ■ ■

"Bernie Boo," "Miss B", "Berdine", "Mrs. Tredwell" – these were her most frequent appellations. I met this woman of many names when I was four years old. But to me, she was always "Momma."

The cohesion of my family of origin had disintegrated some time earlier and I was in foster care on the Eastern Shore. My case worker, Ms. Lipscomb, had arranged a passing site visit to determine the level of physical chemistry between the potential parent and the child.

Momma and my soon-to-be-father, Leon, had no doubt seen pictures of me, but the site visit is often a determining moment. Can the couple see themselves as the authentic parents of this child in the varied venues of their lives? Can they hold up their heads with pride? Can they love unconditionally? Is "coloration" a factor?

Our site visit was scheduled in a public building in downtown Newport News, Virginia in a "fishbowl;" a large playroom with lots of toys and a massive window on a busy hallway, with many people coming and going. I was busy with a toy truck when she opened the door and spoke.

"Hi," she said.

After brief introductions, I smiled at her and spoke, "I know why you are here."

"You do?" she responded.

"Yes," I said boldly. "You are here because you are thinking about adopting me."

Our initial encounter would be told and retold over the next 30 odd years and Momma would always say, "I knew he was mine. Any child that knew at four years of age that I was interested in adopting him was my child!"

The next year, she would take out an insurance policy for my college education. It is important to say that while I may have been cute, adorable, and highly intelligent, I had burned down the foster mother's woodshed. Just sayin'. It was the social worker's responsibility to tell my mother about the fire. Failing to inform prospective adoptive parents of the full behaviors of a foster child would be malpractice.

But to this day, I argue that the whole thing was accidental.

I was playing in the backyard of my foster mother's home and decided to walk into the woodshed. The shed was a probably three-foot by five-foot wooden, enclosed whitewashed structure, with a hinged door and a sloppy lock. On the shelf, were a couple boxes of matches, and hanging in the corner was an old green and white hammock. My sense of creativity at age four suggested that it would be interesting to observe the burning of the fringe on the hammock. So, one by one, I began to light the individual fringes and watched them burn to the base of their attachment to the hammock material, at which point, the first fringes burned out. Except, after a few of those initial burnings, more than one caught fire, and as I tried to blow it out, the fire just got bigger. That approach clearly wasn't working, so I backed out of the woodshed, closed the door, and walked down the alley.

At some point, the flames and the smoke emerging from the wood-filled shed signaled to the nearby community that there was a problem. I only remember two things; the sound of the distant fire engines and the physical beating I received from my foster mother.

The beating was severe, but having to endure the repetitive voice of her birth daughter yelling, "Beat him, Momma, beat him!" was probably more painful.

My next major shenanigan happened after being adopted and presented itself at the Wells family homestead on "A" Avenue in Norfolk.

We three cousins were playing in the backyard. The homestead, my grandparent's home purchased before the Great Depression, was the generational legacy resulting from the tireless work ethic of Henderson and Fannie Wells. Henderson operated his cab as an entrepreneur and Fannie was a household domestic. Their home was a two-story faux-brick shingled dwelling, with an inviting front porch stretching the width of the house. In back, there was a sizable, but poorly groomed yard. The only thing that separated our property from Miss Lucie's, our next-door neighbor, was a chicken wire fence, the kind that had the wide-wire panes large enough to easily put a hand and arm through.

We were acting mischievously, playing doctor. It was my idea, so I set the rules. I boisterously instructed my male and female cousin, "Pants down... shirts up...up against the fence!"

As the doctor in residence, it was my privilege to inspect the two bodies before me, feeling and examining each one, and momentarily rubbing our genitals across each other. Giggling with delight and the freedom of being naked outdoors, doing what we knew was "naughty," yet thoroughly engrossed in our mutual innocent fantasy.

Miss Lucie was casually looking out her back window as she sipped her mid-day cup of coffee, when two naked brown butts pressed against the chicken wire fence caught her attention as probably the most disruptive visual of her morning.

In the 1950's, neighbors were permitted to correct other people's children, particularly within the African American community. But rather than confronting us herself, Miss Lucie got on the mainline, and she wasn't calling Jesus. She phoned my mother, alerting her to the mischief going on in *her* backyard.

As we three enjoyed our play, from out of nowhere, came a force that felt like an approaching thunderstorm, shattering our group fantasy. In her hands, she held a leather belt which seemed to operate with a quickness, back and forth...swish... crack...The screams and the yells and the cries of agony which rose from each of us as the leather connected with our flesh thoroughly exploded any sense of our alternative reality. This corrective, this woman with the strap, was the real world.

"You nasty thangs!" she shrieked.

A few more licks of the belt for the two boys, but several more for the girl, whom she labeled a "strumpet." My cousins were whipped and sent home. I was whipped and confined to my room.

It never seemed to occur to any of the adults that of the three children, one of us had just a little too much information – for a five-year-old. In a matter of another five years or less, I would begin to receive a very different message as to who I was, or at least whom others thought or projected me to be.

My sociological analysis of the Wells/Tredwell clan is that they represented two distinct classes of African American society. My father was from the lower class, the poorest of the poor, living on Cumberland Avenue, the poorest street in the city of Norfolk. My mother was the product of the Black middle class; Black people who owned their own businesses and properties and supported their own churches and fraternal organizations, even during the Great Depression of 1929. Men and women who lived by what Kelly Brown Douglas termed, the "Narrative of Civility."

My father, Leon Charles, was the only son of Charles "Charlie" Tredwell, an African American native of Creswell, North Carolina, who might be considered "high-yellow" in complexion. My grandfather was 6'2" in height, weighed less than 200 pounds, and was a Black veteran of World War I; an experience which gifted him with shrapnel to his head, reducing him to a residual life of ever-impending death. Charlie became an alcoholic.

My Aunt Blanche told the story of how my father would be summoned by word of mouth to come and bring his father home from one of the major Black bars. My father was no more than 5'9", which meant that his father towered over him by five inches, as he held his hand bringing him home through the Black and Jewish business sections of the community. Charlie's home was not the home of my grandmother. "Home" for my grandfather was further down the street at a different woman's dwelling, where he had also seeded and nurtured two other female children.

Aunt Blanche would also tell stories of their poverty and hunger. She told me that at age 16, my father worked setting up pins in the bowling alley after school, before pin automation. Blanche said that the little bit of money that my father earned often made the difference between being able to provide a single meal in a day for his family, or being able to have an additional meal. It is an indisputable fact that the Norfolk division of the Tredwell family had known both intense hunger and steep poverty.

Aunt Blanche was both of our favorites for more reasons than Mother and I could count. She was a beautiful Black woman in her own right, who wore her permed hair long, because Uncle Boe, her husband, loved it that way. While Blanche did not sing, in her carefree moments, she would let out a distinctive whistle. Aunt Blanche and Momma had a special bond.

For reasons beyond my understanding, certain people in Southern Virginia and Northern Carolina seem to love salt-cured Smithfield hams. There was a game akin to tag played between my Aunt Blanche and Momma. Blanche would visit Norfolk from Chicago at least once a year, staying for a week or more, primarily to visit with her mother, MomMatt. I noticed that when Aunt Blanche would leave, she would strategically place an envelope of thanks for Momma for the comfort of her visit. Tucked in her thank-you note would be several 100 dollar bills.

"She didn't have to do this!" Momma would scream year after year, upon discovering Blanche's gift.

When early December rolled around, Blanche would unexpectedly receive a Smithfield ham in the mail. I was convinced of their mutual love for each other. Blanche was always, without question, my favorite aunt. What I did not understand at the time was the often pervasive transactional nature of persons having experienced deep poverty and hunger.

■ ■ ■

Spending Saturday evening together, Daddy was being his normal quiet self, more pensive that usual, but ever the introvert, while Momma and I began making plans for the next morning - worship at Mt. Olive Baptist, the Wells' family church.

I have always loved "Church" and the varying styles of African American worship. Church is where I discovered my music and my earliest speaking voice. I am probably one of the few kids whose worst, unimaginable punishment was to be banned from church on Sunday morning.

It was my responsibility to clean the house on Saturday. In most instances, both my parents were gone from the house that day, and Momma would return around 6 p.m. that evening. She would inspect the mopping, dusting, and vacuuming, with an emphasis on the bathrooms and trash removal. If any dimension of this work did not meet her approval, she would speak to it.

"Looks like you don't want to go to church in the morning, 'cause you didn't empty these trash cans."

I would plead for mercy as I quickly gathered the trash.

When I was ten years of age, Mother and I were standing in the vestibule of Mt. Olive Baptist, just a few blocks from the family homestead. The foyer of the church is tiered, with an initial flooring level with the exterior door, and a second landing up three steps level with the interior flooring. Highly varnished, shiny swinging double doors led into the sanctuary. Mother and I were on the second landing when a middle-aged woman quietly entered from the outside. She was not a member of our church as far as we knew, and we perceived her to be a visitor. According to the operative "Narrative of Civility," one did not talk in the vestibule. The three of us stood in silence for a few moments, when suddenly the guest spoke up.

"Is that your son?" she asked.

"Yes," my mother replied.

"He is anointed," the stranger declared in a voice of spiritual authority. "He is a preacher, anointed and called of God."

As she made this declaration, the woman's body shivered as if the Holy Ghost was moving over her and was, at that very moment, affirming her proclamation. Mother and I looked into each other's eyes in amazement, pondering what had just happened.

An influencing social construct among the membership of Mt. Olive Baptist in the 1950's was the aforementioned "Narrative of Civility," which can be interpreted as a propensity toward western liturgical forms of worship, minimizing and discarding many of the traditional cultural "Africanisms" associated with African American worship.

Mt. Olive's primary musical instrument was a two-tiered pipe organ, the console of which was located just behind the pulpit and in the center of the choir loft. Our choir members wore robes in all seasons; long-flowing robes for men and women in the fall and winter months, with shorter white gowns and caps worn in the heat of the summer. Our pastor held an earned Doctor of Ministry degree.

There was a defined order of worship outlined in the folded bulletin one received upon entrance, coupled with a paper fan generally provided by one of the local prominent funeral homes. There was no "Devotional Service" before worship began. But one of the truest indications of our acculturation beyond our traditional Africanisms was an absence of the "shout" - what Du Bois termed the "frenzy." Well, not a complete absence. For at the turn of the 1960's, there was still one woman who shouted... Sister Walker.

On a very rare Sunday morning, all the youth in or near my age range could be found in the last pew of the church on the left-hand side. As service progressed, we would write notes to each other and fold the pages of the hymnal to construct funny phrases.

One of the youth whispered, "You know Mrs. Walker shouts on the second chorus of the 'Hymn of Invitation.'"

"What?" The group completely rejected that idea.

However, undaunted by our skepticism, the teller of this tale went on to suggest that Sister Walker, also a choir member, was particularly prone to shout on the first Sunday of the month – Communion Sunday.

As we conversed, we realized with delight it was Communion Sunday. Our focus turned to the order of service. Pastor Meyers was about to get up to preach, and the Hymn of Invitation would come next. When Pastor concluded his message and the organist began to play the hymn, all eyes were on the choir loft, specifically on Sister Walker.

The congregation sang the first verse and the first chorus. In the middle of the second verse, the teller of the tale began to count down as we approached the second chorus. "Ten, nine, eight,..."

And on one, Mrs. Walker predictably screamed as if on cue, "Yes Lord! Thank Ya!"

We all doubled over with laughter in our seats. I thought I would bust a gut - damage my being! We were bent over in the pew, enjoying the humor of the moment, even as we tried to suppress any disruptive sound. For the first time in my life, I heard the voice of the Holy Ghost speak to me.

The Spirit said "Why are you laughing at that woman?"

When I heard the question, I began to sober up and realized something greater than I had anticipated was occurring.

The Spirit went on to say, "She's only doing that because I have been good to her."

Then, after a substantive pause, even as the previous words resonated in my heart, the Spirit concluded, "And, I've been good to you too."

In the space of what was likely only a matter of seconds, I experienced a flashback to my abandonment, remembering the violence and trauma that I had experienced, some of which had been blocked from my memory, but ever present in my body. I remembered the dirty streets, the dust, and the absence of grass or anything green growing - not even a tree.

I remembered the day when a gang of men got into a brawl and I could hear afresh as that one injured man was crying, "My eye, my eye," staggering with a bloody face, searching.

I remembered hunting with him, looking down into the dirt and finally seeing that blind eyeball staring upward.

Immediately that day in that pew, in mental contrast, I began to recognize the potential for opportunity and redemption that my adoption represented. I started to feel thankful for my new parents, my new home, and the safe environment that I now so effortlessly enjoyed - and I lost it!

I got up from the pew and began to walk around the back of the church, shouting at the top of my voice, "Jesus, Lord, I thank you. You have surely been good to me!"

On that Communion Sunday, the worship at Mt. Olive witnessed a transcending of the "Narrative of Civility," reaffirming our Africanisms, as a 60-year-old woman shouted from the choir stand and a ten-year-old boy shouted from the back of the church. After that Sunday, my church friends refused to sit with me anymore, afraid of the Spirit. But in that same year, I was elected youth minister by all my peers, as well as by the teens and young adults of the church.

That visiting woman in the vestibule knew something.

■ ■ ■

Mt. Olive was also a musical church. There were two choirs, senior and youth. Among the senior choristers were four soloists whom we deemed exceptional; Mother West, Suzy Hill, Brother Patterson and Deacon Bill Clemmons. Mother West possessed a warm, comforting, sweet melodic soprano voice. She sang "God Leads Us Along:"

In shady green pastures, so rich and so sweet,
God leads His dear children along;
Where the water's cool flow bathes the weary one's feet
God leads His dear children along.

Some, through the waters, some through the flood
Some, through the fire, but all through the blood.
Some, through great trials, but God giveth a song
In the night season, and all the day long.

Sometimes on the mount where the sun shines so bright
God leads His dear children along
Sometimes in the valley, in darkest of night
God leads His dear children along.

Some, through the waters, some through the flood
Some, through the fire, but all through the blood.
Some, through great trials, but God giveth a song
In the night season, and all the day long.

Mother West would lead out the verse in a free-flowing style, *a piacere*, after which the chorus would move into a rhythmic call and response.

Yet, the zenith of the performance would be reached when the words of the chorus were slightly changed into a question, "Have you been through great trials? Have you been through the flood?"

Inevitably, one of the mothers on the Deaconess Board would lift her hand, with tears running down her cheeks, and quietly whisper, "Yes, Lord! Thank you, Jesus."

Suzy Hill, more of a scratchy soprano, would also from time to time render a heart-stirring rendition of "I am Satisfied with Jesus."

> *I am satisfied with Jesus, He has done so much for me,*
> *He has suffered to redeem me, He has died to set me free.*
> *When the question comes to me, as I think of Calvary.*
> *Is my Master satisfied with me?*
> *I am satisfied, I am satisfied, I am satisfied with Jesus.*
> *When the question comes to me, as I think of Calvary,*
> *Is my Master, satisfied with me?*

Brother Patterson, a round-bellied shorter man with a rich baritone voice sang "He Will Remember Me:"

> *When on the cross of Calvary, the Lord was crucified,*
> *A mob stood round about Him,*
> *And mocked Him till He died.*
> *Two Thieves were nailed beside Him,*
> *To share the agony,*

But one of them, cried out to Him,
Oh Lord! Remember me.
Oh, will the Lord remember me, when I am called to go?
When I have crossed death's chilly sea, will He His love there
show?
Oh, Yes! (Yes, Yes) He heard my feeble cry,
From bondage set me free...
And when I reach the pearly gates,
He will remember me!"

But, the "hot chocolate" was not truly served until the Nat King Cole of the church, Deacon Bill Clemmons, a tall, handsome, honey brown man, rose from his seat in the choir stand and lifted his velvety smooth tenor voice to sing, in solo, "Jesus, Savior, Pilot Me:"

Jesus, Savior, pilot me,
Over life's tempestuous sea,
Unknown waves, around me roll,
Hiding rock, and treacherous shoal
Chart and compass, come from thee
Jesus, Savior, pilot me.

As a mother stills her child,
Thou canst hush the ocean wild
Boisterous waves obey Thy will
When Thou say'st to them be still
Wonderous Sovereign of the sea,

Jesus, Savior, pilot me.

At Deacon Clemmons' conclusion, there was seldom a dry eye in the congregation.

In reflecting upon my early musical mentors today, decades later, I can recite their songs almost word for word. Yet, I only remember one sermon preached in all my early years between the age of 10 and 16. In many ways, I think this speaks profoundly to the role of Black music in the theological underpinnings of the historical Black Church. From hush harbors, where their pots were turned upside down to muffle the sounds of their song, to two-tiered pipe organs, instruments never designed with gospel music in mind.

The one sermon I remember from this period was preached by a guest minister from out of town. His sermon was entitled *The Fathers Have Eaten the Sour Grapes, and the Children's Teeth Have Been Set on Edge!* (Jeremiah 31:29)

2

The Lord is my Shepherd, I Shall not Want.
—Traditional

Ten years of age was, for me, the point in time to have a brief, but serious, conversation with Momma. We were in a moment of mutual comforting; deescalating our heightened emotions, having successfully lifted our drunk respective father and husband from the living room floor to the bedroom just down the hall. Urine and feces-filled pants considered, it was a messy job, but according to Momma, it was our responsibility to do.

She and I were now seated in the dining room in the two Mediterranean black leather chairs next to the Mediterranean china cabinet. I was crying from emotional exhaustion. How could I protect my cup of joy, which was three-quarters full, yet so very vulnerable to these intermittent incidents of trauma and their destructiveness?

As we gently rocked each other, I whispered to Momma, "You know, we don't have to live this way...You are smart, I'm smart...We can make it without Daddy."

She did not hear my plea for stability. Rather, she thought that I wanted her all to myself.

"Your Daddy has an illness, and if we leave him, he won't ever get any better," she replied.

What I didn't fully understand was not only Momma's undying devotion to Daddy, but also her enmeshment with the Narrative of Civility: True virtuous Black ladies don't marry more than once, widowhood being an exception. Momma had been married before to a man with the last name of Rogers. That was one of the contentions Leon's sisters, Pooh and Lucy, held against Momma when he announced to his family his plans to marry her.

It is important to remember that Pooh and Lucy were "blues women;" women who understood and maneuvered the context of Cumberland Avenue, the behaviors exhibited on Church Street, and the survival strategies employed on Brambleton Avenue. The Wells family and their children were known within the African American community. Pooh and Lucy would seek out "the word on the street" as to who Momma was and the nature of her previous marriage. They did this particularly once she began to date their brother.

According to the family rumor mill, this Tredwell family discussion got heated until Daddy cursed and said, "Dammit! I'm marrying Berdine, and that's that!"

Daddy almost never cursed and would never intentionally curse in front of his mother, MomMatt. The girls knew they had lost the argument – for that moment at least.

Unbeknownst to me, there was another driving force aiding Momma's co-dependency; markings that were in my face for a quarter of a century, yet never fully disclosed. These markings she took to her grave, with many years passing before time and my lived experience surfaced their meaning. As I think on it, that scar on her breastbone, and those missing front teeth, were never fully explained. Somehow, Momma's argument and willingness to be co-dependent was not persuasive to me.

Things blew up one night in a very similar scene to the one when I was ten. The major difference was that I was now 16 and my frustration felt like a staggering whirlwind. I felt trapped, stifled. I was completely unaware of the concept of ambivalence, though in retrospect that is one descriptor. I was as unaware of ambivalence as my father was of his post-traumatic stress disorder. I loved my father, but these continuing episodes wore me out. I was just tired; tired of being teased by my peers, tired of this repeating trauma.

As Momma and I were standing above Daddy, positioning ourselves to lift him, instead of lifting, I began to kick him as hard as I could and in as many places as I could. My simmer was now at a boil. I was so emotionally drained; I could hardly keep my head on straight. With each kick came some deplorable descriptor of what he was and what he was not. Is it better to be raised in a place where nothing grows, where your destiny is doomed? Or to live in a context where one's cup of joy is three-quarters full, knowing it will be pissed in every six to eight weeks?

Dr. Newby, our family physician and counselor, suggested that I be placed outside of the home for some extended period of time.

Momma to the rescue. She wanted me to be placed within the family. She also wanted me to be under the tutelage of a straight man in hopes of correcting some of my "wayward" sexual expressions. To whom could Momma describe her family melt-down and who would really understand? Who would care enough about her and this adopted boy to care for him for "some extended period of time?" The answer to all of this was Aunt Blanche. Blanche and her husband, Boe.

Perfect, because Momma had cared for Blanche's mother and "fair exchange is not robbery." So... youthfully handsome, with varied sexual interest, budding musical talent, one led by the Holy Ghost, and given to shout...I was off to Chicago in the spring of 1966.

In retrospect, there was so much that I did not know about African American people living in Chicago; the richness of their history and their varied contributions to the context of the city. I was unknowingly walking into the final decade of the Great Northern Migration; a 60-year-long movement of African Americans from Southern cities and states to Northern metropolises like New York and Chicago. I would learn more about the musical and spiritual traditions of the South in Chicago than I had ever encountered in Virginia, the home of the Confederacy.

Blanche and Boe were approaching their 25th wedding anniversary when I entered their lives full-time. There had been fertility issues in their early years, probably the result of the absence of appropriate aftercare following a miscarriage in Blanche's first marriage. One of the many things I loved about her is she made it a point to speak to me about life and the lived experience, drawing from her own story. A second initiative Aunt Blanche began was to let me make my own decisions.

Regardless of the situation, she would say, "It's your decision to make!"

I hated this new parenting style at first, but grew to love it over time for the freedom and self-responsibility it came to represent.

So, without coaxing, she would share her lived experience. She gave me a glimpse of her first marriage. She never mentioned his name, but evidently, they met in Norfolk and were quickly married. She said they were in their honeymoon season and her female elders, Aunt Hattie and her mother, Mattie (MomMatt), decided to take a short trip to Creswell, North Carolina, their geographical place of origin. Aunt Blanche was invited to go along.

She said to me that she was glad for the opportunity to get away from her new husband, because quietly she confessed, "He was a man...a real man!"

The implication centered on the wealth of his endowment, and then, in a weary voice she whispered, "He had worn me out."

I snickered quietly, hoping she would say even more, but told myself to be satisfied with what she had shared. This idea of having open sexual discussions with an adult was more than I had anticipated in this new context. Whew!

Aunt Blanche said she and the other women took the Greyhound bus and she felt that there was something about the physical roughness of this over-the-road trip that dislodged the conceived embryo. She shared that when she got to the outhouse behind the Lewis homestead, there was nothing but blood, more blood than she had ever seen. Decades later, she and Uncle Boe would conceive and produce a son, Junior, who was eight years old when I arrived.

My Uncle Boe was born and raised in a small farming town outside of Atlanta, Georgia. At the age of 18, he entered the Navy as a prelude to his upward mobility. He was at least 6'4" in height and probably weighed 275 pounds. His coloring was close to a honey brown with yellow undertones. His mother could have passed for a white woman, while his father had the coloring of a hickory nutshell.

I had met Uncle Boe once before, only for a day, the Sunday of MomMatt's funeral. He was overtly a loving man. Balding slightly, so he wore his hair close to his head. He was the first man I met who required custom shoes; his feet may have been size 18. To compliment his custom shoes, he wore custom suits. This was natural for him, as after his service in the Navy, he attended a tailoring school.

Once in Chicago, that seed of tailoring would lead him into the dry cleaning business. He and his cousin, Ervin, created Ervin and Lee Cleaning and Tailoring. When I arrived, there were two locations: the main plant on 51st and Indiana, and a drop off/pick up location on Garfield and 55th Street, not far from Dr. Martin Luther King, Jr. Drive.

My first lesson learned on arriving in Chicago was to understand that people in the Ervin and Lee family worked, and they worked hard. Uncle Boe was among the hardest-working. He would leave the house before 7 a.m. Monday through Saturday and would generally not return home until 9 or 10 p.m. He would then shower and go to bed.

Boe managed the cleaning and pressing functions and was the chief engineer responsible for fixing any breakdowns or failures of equipment. There were at least four full-time employees at the 51st Street location. Blanche worked full-time, managing the two part-time employees at Garfield.

Mr. Ervin had a day job as well, after which he would come to the plant and press clothes. His wife, Aunt Nita, sewed piece work at a factory off 35th and Fleshing Street until 4:30 p.m., after which she would come to the Garfield location and handle any heavy sewing and clothing repairs.

Nita was born and raised in New Orleans. Not only could she sew, she could cook - to the point where one might strain themselves in consumption. Talk about "feed me until I want no more," which is exactly what I did on my first Thanksgiving dinner at the Ervin house. Once I left the table, I could not sit up, and had to lay down on the floor until things settled. A 16-year-old greedy spectacle!

The Lee's were people of faith, longstanding members of Ebeneezer Missionary Baptist Church, located at 45th Street and Vincennes Avenue, where Uncle Boe taught Sunday school and Aunt Blanche would faithfully sit, Sunday after Sunday, on the far right side of the church near the deacons.

After many years of teaching young boys about Christ and tithing faithfully, Uncle Boe was elevated to the Diaconate. He was never verbose. Whenever he spoke, his words were few. And if that did not capture you, the softness of his tone compelled you to listen. Uncle Boe was a man of great wisdom. He was referred to by the church members as "The Gentle Giant."

Ebeneezer is a historic African American church in the city of Chicago. Founded in 1902, having split from Olivet Missionary Baptist Church, the oldest African American church in the city. The Reverend J.F. Thomas led a group of some 30 individuals to form Ebenezer Missionary Baptist after a raucous disagreement regarding the acquisition of a plot of land. In 1920, after worshiping in several locations, the pastor and deacons met with Isaiah Temple, a Jewish Synagogue, regarding the acquisition of their property on 45th and Vincennes. Terms of the agreement: a purchase price of $65,000, with a down payment of $26,000.

But it was Ebenezer's third pastor, Reverend James Howard Lorenzo Smith, who envisioned the secret recipe that would cause the church membership to increase to over 3000, and for the church to be known as "The Birthplace of Gospel Music." Nine months into his pastorate, Smith proclaimed his vision of a mass choir seated behind the pulpit that would sing "songs of the spiritual forefathers down in the Southland."

Pastor Smith was, in fact, calling for the organization of Ebenezer's first gospel choir, and in this accomplishment, birthing the first gospel choir in the city of Chicago. In December of that same year, Smith brought together musicians and gospel composers Theodore Frye and Thomas Dorsey. After a month of rehearsals, The Ebenezer gospel choir made its debut to a packed house; the church seats over a thousand people. The creation of a senior choir, junior choir, and junior gospel choir, also known as the youth choir, followed. Wait for it...I would join the youth choir.

Six weeks after forming the Ebenezer gospel choir, Thomas Dorsey, the father of gospel music, left Ebenezer's piano keys and moved to Pilgrim Baptist Church to form their first gospel choir. He was replaced by Roberta Martin, a "Daughter of Ebenezer" and another gospel giant.

After a few years, Ms. Martin left Ebenezer to start the Roberta Martin Singers. Ebenezer's celebrated music department contributed to the shaping of musical greats, including Dinah Washington, Edward Colvin, Willie Brown, Willa Mae Ford Smith, Robert Anderson, Milt Hinton, Willie Webb, Delois Barrett Campbell, Billie Barrett Greenbey, the Norfleet Brothers, Theodore Charles Stone, Sallie Martin and Ethelynde Armstrong Engram.

During my brief tenure at Ebenezer, I was fortunate to glimpse many of these gospel giants during Roberta Martin's annual concert that she produced out of gratitude for Ebenezer's support of her musical development. At some earlier point, the church had paid for her piano lessons.

I discovered my own music abilities back in Norfolk at the age of 13, initiated and motivated by a particular gospel song, "Peace be Still," released by the Reverend James Cleveland and the Angelic Gospel Choir in 1963. Cleveland taught Aretha Franklin to play the piano.

My allowance for cleaning the house was $1.50 a week, so I negotiated a deal with my choir director, Ms. Macklin. I would pay her 75 cents for the piano lesson. I bought the lesson book, and the first song, "Swans on the Lake," was a gentle, calming, one-note-at-a-time piece. The concluding notes of the final measure suggested that harmonies might be possible...but not quite yet.

About that same time, I fell in love with Rosemont Junior High School's theme song, taken from a hymn, "Be Still My Soul." I was working on that from our church hymn book when Ms. Macklin and I met again. I played my "Swans on the Lake" and I mentioned to her I was also practicing this hymn. Upon her request, I played "Be Still My Soul" without much difficulty. As she listened, she was cool as a cucumber, and only gave me my next assignment. We parted in peace.

Unbeknownst to me, Ms. Macklin made a call to Bernie Boo suggesting my teacher needed to be one who had broader musical capacities, able to engage the musical genres of classical, jazz, standards, blues, and gospel. Ms. Macklin's recommendation was Professor Robert Nance (his name has been changed to protect the guilty and the innocent). Dr. Nance's musical qualifications were impeccable. However, there was one caveat - the word on the street was, though married to a woman, Dr. Nance was rumored to be bisexual.

Boo already had well-established concerns regarding my sexuality. From her perspective, to "put me in the lion's mouth" might not be the best parental move.

She would say regarding Queerness, "That's not what I want for you! I want you to know a 'woman's love.'"

Let me say in the vernacular of Doris Day, "Honey, 'Que sera, sera: Whatever will be, will be.'"

Subsequently, piano lessons dissipated given this conundrum. It felt like the talent may have been stymied. Perhaps snipped and pruned.

■ ■ ■

Within a few Sundays at Ebenezer, I was transferred from my uncle's class to that of Mr. McFarlane, a middle-aged African American with a high-yellow complexion - married, a classy dresser, with spiffy eyeglasses, and a slightly effeminate affect. He too had roots in the South and had migrated to Chicago. Rumor had it that he was a masseuse in a sports club for mostly white males.

In any event, the church's monthly financial statement said that he was a substantive tither to the church. He and Uncle Boe were in the same category, tithing $50 a week, about $200 a month. It was also in those first weeks in Chicago that Unc demonstrated his caring nature by connecting me with one of his former Sunday school students, Richard. Richard had Unc's full endorsement.

"He's a great young man, clean cut, studious, comes from a great family. He's a musician and he loves the Lord!"

Well, I can't say that it was love at first sight, but somewhere between the second and third blinks, I was smitten. And if looks were not enough, he was the pianist for the youth choir. Sweet Jesus!

Within a few weeks after our initial introduction, one Tuesday after school, Richard showed up at our three-flat. I did not know that Richard was coming over, but if he must, he must!

The Lee's first home was an all-brick three-flat structure near 67th and Paxton. The top two apartments were designed with large picture windows in the front, full living and dining rooms, two bedrooms, a spacious kitchen, one full bath, and a two-car garage. The basement apartment was a utilitarian space, housing several stored pieces of furniture along with the washer and dryer.

The single bedroom was toward the front of the unit. After having slept in Junior's room for the first couple of months, I asked to move to the basement apartment. Junior was one of those children who sang and rocked himself to sleep, which worked my nerves and kept me awake. It was a good move for both of us.

There was a back door entrance to the basement, and in the front, there were two sets of steps separated by a landing wide enough to fit a spinet piano which I rented for $35 per month.

Richard was two years my senior, beginning his freshman year of college at a downtown university. His major, of course, was music, with concentrations in pipe organ and piano. Richard was strikingly handsome, about 5'10" and maybe 155 pounds. His glistening walnut coloring was accentuated by a jet-black mustache and heavy-set eyebrows, accentuated by horn-rimmed glasses. His brown eyes would flash a certain glint when he smiled, and even moreso when he laughed. His beautiful white teeth were all in alignment. Richard was an un-initiated African Prince by every measure. We knew, probably he more than I, that we had to be careful regarding any disclosure of our mutual affection.

But we were teens and by its very definition – silly! We invented special words for our greetings and departures. "Suazooki dude," spoken in a de-meaning intonation, meant "I love you." Additionally, we had a high-pitched scream that we would shriek when we were a block or so apart. And then there were the love letters to each other, two-page minimum.

Several years later, he said all our friends in the choir knew we were lovers, but I never got that sense. One reason was that we both had girlfriends. Co-incidentally, they were both named Linda. I think that he was more uncom-fortable initiating affection with his Linda than I was with mine. He had more clarity regarding his sexuality. His Linda was quiet, unassuming, and demure in her affect, while my Linda was South Side Chicago Hot!

■ ■ ■

I will defend to the death the power and mystic of the African American oral tradition. Yet, one of its challenges within the culture is that some im-portant information gets passed down, and some important information evades dissemination. For example, the names of Tinley, Dorsey, and Frazer did not filter into the knowledge base of the youth choir at Ebenezer. Howev-er, the name Professor Robert Rogers certainly did.

Professor Rogers came to Ebenezer Missionary Baptist Church after the dust created by the historical gospel musicians had settled. Rogers was a gift-ed musician in his own right, possessing a very special quality to both engage and inspire. Everybody loved him. The gospel choir's stand was always filled with 90 to 100 voices, producing a sound that lifted the spirit of all within the sanctuary, singing to a full congregation of over 1000 worshippers each week.

Rogers was so loved that the choir and the church leadership decided to honor the professor with a banquet.

Now, a Black Church Chicago-style banquet is no small affair. The first consideration is the facility. Black prestigious churches, like Ebenezer and Mt. Olivet, held their banquets in downtown Chicago at one of the high-quality hotels, or at a convention center like McCormick Place. Fliers with a picture of the honoree would be inserted in the Sunday bulletin at least four weeks before the event, outlining the date, time, and ticket price.

Black Baptist ladies did not wear too many sequins and beads for worship, but a banquet was different. It was an occasion for formal attire. An occasion for "putting on the dog." Black gentlemen were required to borrow or rent a tuxedo. A banquet presented the opportunity to go to places one normally did not visit, dressed in the formal fashion of the day, and acting out our middle-class longings.

After much preparation by many, the Friday night of the banquet arrived. Needless to say, all who could, as well as "Lottie, Dottie, and everybody" were in attendance. At first, the leadership team thought that the honoree was simply a little late in arriving. So, they proceeded with the program; the welcome, opening prayer, and the blessing of the food, after which the serving of the first course began.

Simultaneously and quietly, a small delegation of the deacons were sent to the South Side to find the good professor. When they finally found him, he was in the intensive care unit of the hospital. The word on the street was that he and his male lover had gotten into a dispute earlier that evening and his lover had beaten the professor within an inch of his life. Escandalo!

Richard and I sought to stay below the radar – on the down-low.

Ebenezer's youth choir was directed by Ms. Payne, a beautiful Black woman with almond colored skin and jet black hair which she wore shoulder-length and straightened with curls. She was in her early 30s, strikingly beautiful, shapely, married, and without children at that juncture. Ms. Payne didn't need a choir to bring the Holy Ghost into the room. Girlfriend could sing. I don't mean could carry a tune – I mean SING! Not only was her voice full and her pitch on point, she could produce a shimmering in her voice that would light up the whole church. And when she had given the song her best, she would join in with the rest of the church and give vent to the presence of the Holy Ghost.

There were approximately 25 to 30 voices in the youth choir and generally we sang in three-part harmony; soprano, alto, and tenor. And like every choir, we had our theme song. For us, it was a song we sang with some frequency. I was often moved to shout when we sang it, unless for some reason the performance was lackluster. We never knew which song we were going to sing until just before we stood up. One Sunday, just as we stood, Ms. Payne announced that theme song, "Beams of Heaven." You could feel every choir member's heart drop.

"Can't believe we have to sing this again! Nevertheless, we can get through it."

We started out with the first line, and by the time we got to the second, something about the song and the sound we were producing felt completely different. The Holy Ghost had entered. By the time we repeated the second chorus, tears began to fall, shoulders began to shake, hands began to be lifted, and newer harmonies began to be heard. When we sang the last five words, immediately there was a spiritual explosion.

Some members fell backwards, landing in their seats, sobbing profusely. Other members began to walk in the aisles as they vocalized praises unto God. Some stood and waved their hands, almost unable to speak. The congregation exploded as well. To see their Black young people; sons and daughters, nephews and nieces, 16 to 20 years of age, acknowledging the power of the Holy Ghost affirmed their successful generational transfer of the Faith and the journey, in ways that are almost beyond expression. Here are the words:

Beams of Heaven, as I go
Through this wilderness below,
Guide my feet, in peaceful ways
Turn my mid-night into days.
I do not know, how long t'will be
Nor what the future holds for me
But this I know, if Jesus leads me
I shall get home, someday

Harder yet, may be the fight
Right may often yield to might,
Wickedness a while may reign
Satan's cause may seem to gain.
There is a God, who rules above.
With hand of might and heart of Love
And if I'm right, He'll fight my battles.
I shall be free, someday.

3

If you're talking 'bout Jesus...He's a friend of mine.
—Traditional

My greatest challenge when I entered my new Chicago context and experience was a place called Englewood High School. We lived near 67th and
Paxton. The means of transport was a bus ride back to 63rd Street, and then an
"L" ride further south and west to the school. The thrill of the "L" ride was that
sharp curve and lean that the train took just before my stop. While I always
felt some relief arriving and departing the station, I also knew that this ride
was the least of my considerations for the day.

In the Fall of 1966, I began my junior year. I tried out for the chancel choir, a
choral group renowned throughout the city. The good news was that I made
the cut, becoming a member of the baritone section. The bad news, I did not
feel connected to anyone among its 30 members. Perhaps even more impactful, I was not even connected to the other young Black males in the baritone
section. I had not found an entrance. I was the new guy in town, with no roots
in the city, no knowledge of the three distinct dress codes among high school
males. Who was I?

Sexual expression is always a thought in the back of the minds of Black
males, particularly within the Arts. Needless to say, the prevalent behavioral

approach of young Black males of Englewood was "hardness." There was very little about me that reflected that. At best, I was considered "nerdy," and most likely suspected to be gay.

Somewhere between my isolation and softness, small groups of Black males would periodically assault me. These attacks would generally happen during lunch. I never ate in the cafeteria, but rather walked a few blocks to a deli or bakery to find a snack. I was most vulnerable on the walk back to school, particularly if there were no other people on the street at the time.

The first time it happened, I sensed the three guys behind me and heard them as they picked up their pace. I thought they were simply going to run around me. No such luck. One kicked me in the back of my leg, while another swung toward my face.

It was on.

I heard one declare, "Give us your money!"

I tussled for a while, looking for an opportunity to run, and when it came, I took off.

After this, I developed a strategy which worked very well. I would carry 25 to 30 coins in my right pocket, mostly pennies, with a few nickels and dimes. When the moment of truth occurred and the demand articulated, I would reach in my pocket, grab the handful of coins, and throw them down on the sidewalk. Inevitably, the attackers would lunge to collect the coins, providing the diversion I needed to escape. "Feet don't fail me now."

■ ■ ■

Chancel rehearsal was conducted early in the morning, before classes started. I did well when the section was called to sing its part. However, when the individual tests were given, I would fail, somewhere between my lack of connection and my own insecurity. I eventually dropped out.

However, one redeeming quality of that Englewood experience was my English teacher, Ms. Powell. Sara Jordan Powell, to be exact. That same year, when Roberta Martin gave her free concert of appreciation at Ebenezer, Ms. Jordan was one of the soloists. I almost fell out of my chair with astonishment. Wow! And could she "sang"– whew! Ms. Jordan was a coloratura soprano, the highest voice of all sopranos and treble voices. She was a slight-statured, light-skinned woman with dark hair, fine facial features and a heartwarming smile.

With Roberta Martin on the keys, Ms. Jordan stepped to the edge of the grand piano to a single microphone. She wore a three-piece suit of winter white, with a matching white felt rhinestone hat. In the awe of everyone, she opened her mouth and sang "In My Heart This Melody of Love Divine:"

Though some may sing to pass the weary night along,
Though some may sing to entertain a worldly throng,
I sing because I worship God in song,
It's in my heart, it's in my heart.

It's in my heart this melody of love divine,
It's in my heart since I am His and He is mine,
It's in my heart, how can I help but sing and shine,
It's in my heart, it's in my heart.

It's in my heart this melody of love divine,
It's in my heart, for I am His and He is mine,
It's in my heart, I can not help but sing and shine,
It's in my heart, it's in my heart.

Ms. Jordan sang the first verse and repeated the chorus twice. As she walked away from the mic, she appeared to be returning to her seat as if her rendition was concluded. The crowd clapped enthusiastically, even as Roberta Martin continued to play and exposit the song's meaning. Then, unexpectedly, Ms. Jordan rose to her feet from her seat and began to sing the second verse, this time without her hat, tossing her shoulder-length permed hair as she returned to the microphone:

> *You ask me why I know His blood can cleanse alone,*
> *You ask me why I know He sits upon the throne,*
> *And why I know He chose me for His own,*
> *It's in my heart, it's in my heart.*

The church went up – and so did I.

Now that I knew Ms. Jordan was a Believer, I decided to tell her that I was at the concert and how much I enjoyed her performance. I wondered if she would answer a question for me. I had recently run into a member of the Jehovah Witnesses who told me that only 144,000 people will go to heaven. I asked her if this was true.

"They didn't read far enough," she responded with that loving smile. "If you keep on reading, the author says he saw another group of people bound for heaven, a number of people who could not be counted. These were they, who had come up through hard trials and tribulations, and had their robes washed in the blood of the lamb!"

And then she added, "You and I are in that number!"

That right there was good enough for me.

If Richard had these types of Theological or biblical questions, he never expressed them to me. He was very much all about his music, following the adage that if you find something that you do well – do that! He was, and is, a Black musical genius. He never talked about his first year in college or what he felt for Linda, if anything. I think it's fair to say that it was not easy for him to express his emotions. His sexual expression was the exception. We held a strong passion for each other – perhaps because we were first lovers to each other.

There are many thresholds that one crosses in declaring and owning one's Queerness, even at a young age. It feels like entering some slightly alternative reality. The rules and constructs of this initial reality are present, but somehow appear to lose their potency. This new experience compels one to redefine previous understandings with new realities, realities hidden from common view. The experience is most profoundly a revealer of truths; truths often hidden from the self, yet that demand recognition of their existence.

I loved Richard then, and I love him now. Now, more as a treasured memory and experience that sought to bring me closer to my truest self.

Tuesdays after school, he would come by the three-flat on Paxton. We almost always observed our ritual of playing songs for each other, after which we would make love. Richard was more sensitive than I, and it was not unusual for us to chill for a moment, allowing some of the passion to recede, and in turn, allowing for a more prolonged experience.

One Tuesday evening, we were just settling into our lovemaking when we heard the back door to the apartment opening and the sound of Aunt Blanche's whistle. Richard went into complete panic. I just pantomimed that we be absolutely still, pull the sheets up over our heads, and breathe normally. I thought if she came through the back door, maybe she would also leave that same way and not come through the apartment.

I was wrong. She came through the apartment and up the front stairs, passing the piano and walking out the front door. She never stopped or appeared to glance into my bedroom. We heard her ring of keys open and then lock the front door. The encounter was too close a call for Richard, who quickly jumped up and dressed, wanting to get away from this scene as quickly as possible.

In a few months, our love for each other would be discovered with neither of us being present, in the flesh.

For Christmas that year, Aunt Blanche and Uncle Boe gave me a tape recorder. They reasoned that with my vocal and piano interest, this would be a good tool to assist in my development. I received the gift well before December 25, because I was going home to Norfolk for the holiday.

I was of course glad to see Momma and she was very glad to see me. Daddy was polite, but stoic. I don't remember any negative incidents during this holiday. What I didn't realize was that while things were quiet in Norfolk, life-changing drama was occurring back in Chicago.

Aunt Blanche told the story this way: At some point during the holidays, she entertained a few of her friends. And, at some juncture in their conversation, someone asked about me. Blanche mentioned that they had given me a recorder for my birthday and how much I enjoyed it. I had left the recorder in their apartment for security of mind. Blanche wanted to demonstrate the recorder, but couldn't find the mic so they could try it. She figured it was probably downstairs, so she searched the piano stool and then my room looking for the mic. She found the gold and black box in which the recorder came and opened it. The mic wasn't there, but she found something else - the love letters.

"I smiled and wondered which one of your girlfriends was writing you love letters," Blanche had recalled.

So, she opened the first letter and read it. When she saw the closing signature, "Love, Richard," she said her heart dropped.

Sometime after the first of January, I flew into Midway Terminal. Aunt Blanche picked me up.

I didn't perceive any difference in her demeanor until she said, "I have something I have to tell you. While you were away..."

She proceeded to reiterate the story in all its detail.

My response was, "I'm surprised you let me return."

Aunt Blanche told me she had some trepidation, but when she saw me get off the plane and walk toward the terminal, she realized that she still loved me. I was shaken to my core.

I'm sure that Blanche discussed her findings with Momma, so basically, I was involuntarily out to my family. Although there was never any open discussion, I suspect that the adults wanted to believe that this was a phase, and given time, my hetero-genes would emerge and come to dominate.

With this information upon my return, I wanted to be perceived as a better person than I had been, even before I had begun my "indefinite period of time" in Chicago. At the end of the school year, I returned to Norfolk for the summer and then to begin my senior year of high school there in the fall.

After I was back, I reconnected with several of my old friends, got a summer job in a pickle factory, and in September, joined the 1968 graduating class of Norview High School.

Pickle production, like sausage and hot dog making, is best left undiscussed. The pickle factory experience consumed my entire summer. It gave me a thorough education concerning the metric of volume for a given commodity at harvest. The job also presented an opportunity for financial gain, both in management and its labor force. Above all, it taught me the importance of time and timing, and the economic lessons were of great importance.

For example, it's amazing what 20 hours of overtime does to your weekly pay-check – a "40-hour work week" at $7.50 an hour blossoms into an increase of 75 percent.

This continuing demand of one's time also prevented any major opportunities for expenditures. We worked every day, Monday through Sunday, though the Sunday hours were the shortest. My end of summer reward was to buy my first Hart Schaffner Marx men's suit.

■ ■ ■

While the Brown Supreme Court decision of 1954 legally desegregated public schools, implementation did not begin in Norfolk, Virginia until around 1965. In the fall of that year, Black boys and girls were afforded the opportunity to attend Norview Junior High School, a facility less than 10 blocks from our home in Coronado. In the opposite direction, there was the all-Black Rosemont Junior High that was about 20 blocks away. I had attended Rosemont briefly in the 8th grade, and then transferred to Norview, as did several of my friends.

Hetero-normativity was alive and on display at Norview Junior High. At Rosemont, we were not allowed to hold hands in the hallways between classes. I had no girlfriend at this point, so the rule was without meaning. However, at Norview, these white students were not just holding hands, they could be found in any number of intimate encounters, vertically pressed against the lockers while engaging in passionate kissing that would bring sweat to one's brow. Black students, new to the context, began to emulate this newfound freedom, but strangely, in the twinkling of an eye, this behavior was outlawed.

This was my first contextual introduction to whiteness; the constructs and ideologies that privilege white skin, culture, and historical contributions above all other communities. It is important to note that the teachers and administrative staff were not integrated. Therefore, we had a situation where 13 and 14-year-old Black students were brought into a less than welcoming environment; into authorities and a system that they knew little about. And what they did know, they only knew from a distance, and now found themselves face-to-face with a system in which they were expected to study, absorb, socialize, and thrive, despite the fights with white boys on the way home.

My greatest social challenge that year occurred when Daddy took a job as one of the janitors. I would come out of school at the end of the day with my Black friends and he would be emptying trash cans or engaging in some other menial job.

At first, my friends would ask, "Isn't that your Daddy?"

I would proudly answer, "Yes."

If close enough, I would speak to him. I had matured. I knew what they didn't know; that in six-to-eight weeks, this embarrassing situation would be over. Gordon Gin would see to that. And it was so.

In Chicago, I passed my junior year, but with less than a stellar performance. Perhaps, that's why the high school counselor in my senior year back in Norfolk thought that a vocational track of study was appropriate for me. When my turn came to meet with her, she expressed some significant reservation as to whether I was "college material."

My response to her was, "Oh no, I have to be on the academic track, because when I was five-years-old, my mother took out an insurance policy for my college education."

She looked at me, wide-eyed. I returned her gaze with polite certainty, and we agreed on the academic track.

■ ■ ■

When I returned to Norfolk, I did not return to Mount Olive Baptist Church, but rather joined a small Pentecostal church, New Hope Church of God in Christ, within walking distance from our home. In fact, it was a stone's throw from Norview High School. This would be my introduction to some new religious concepts - the baptism in the Holy Ghost and dancing in the Spirit.

My musical skills would be significantly challenged as well, as their top musicians produced a musical sound that resided somewhere between traditional gospel and jazz. Nevertheless, I was eventually hired as one of the musicians for the youth choir. Additionally, I was instructed to fast and pray. During certain periods of time, the entire church would fast as a community, not taking in one morsel of food from morning until the evening meal. Momma didn't like this idea, but she went along with the program. We were instructed to make chicken soup to break the fast and avoid heavy meals. Momma shook her head, but she made the soup for me.

The order of worship was not that different from the Baptist. We sang a hymn of the morning, followed by Scripture reading and altar prayer. After that, the choir serving that Sunday would render a special selection, followed by the announcements, then a song before the message preached by Pastor Elder Herman Clark. Dr. Clark, as he became to be known, was a spiritually powerful, sincere man of God. He preached to exposit the Word of God and did not interject issues of politics or social matters. He simply and profoundly interpreted the Scriptures. It was believed that faithfulness to the Scriptures in our daily walk with God would somehow resolve all of the major issues of our lives, and they would be resolved to our good.

This church believed that sin was to be avoided at all costs, that all men and women are sinners, and all need to repent from their sins and turn to God. In turning to God, every man and woman needed to receive the baptism in the Holy Ghost with the evidence of speaking in unknown tongues. This baptism was a seal upon the soul of the individual, sealing them to the day of redemption; either death or the second coming of Christ.

Given my religious fervor, I of course wanted to receive this baptism. I had already received water baptism at Mount Olive, but I was willing to be baptized again, if necessary. I was instructed to come to the "Tarry Service" held on Wednesday nights, where the Saints gather and tarry before the Lord to be filled with the Holy Ghost.

The first hour-and-a-half consisted of constant prayer on our knees, while we repeatedly called on the name, "Jesus! Jesus, Jesus, Jesus," breathe..."Jesus, Jesus, Jesus," breathe, etc., until eventually one's speech stammers, which is considered stammering tongues, which in some religious communities equates to speaking in tongues.

As young people, we were competing to receive this Divine Blessing. There was a young songstress named Jane, who led a number of different songs in the youth choir. However, her attitude was not always the best. In fact, given some of her interactions, it wasn't clear if Jane was a Believer. In one particular tarry service, Jane got caught up in the prayer, while the rest of us, through eye-to-eye contact, watched what was unfolding and heard the change in her voice. In a matter or minutes, after an hour of prayer, she began to speak in tongues.

Now, this was no small miracle because anyone who knew anything about her, knew she was not a faker. If she tarried and got the Holy Ghost, it was a genuine experience – it was real. But, the ultimate evidence of the baptism in the Holy Ghost was to experience a change in our behaviors and our lives, especially visible in how we treated others. Now that Jane had been filled, would she treat people better? Unfortunately, over time, this evidence proved to be lacking. What did that say about the experience, and what did that say about Jane?

A cultural and spiritual challenge for me was that I had been Baptist all my life and I had acquired a sense of the presence of the Holy Ghost only in quieter, slower, often mournful melodic songs such as "Amazing Grace" or "Just as I Am."

Pentecostal worship is blessed with a capacity to encompass many emotions and just as many poly-rhythms in a single communal gathering. My problem was that I could not feel the Spirit in the more intense rhythms. When the Saints would break out into the dance, I did not feel the Holy Ghost. Not only was this outside of my learned and lived cultural vocabulary, I was literally without language to ground this experience. How does one express what my gathered community was feeling and what I was feeling?

In a few months, I would come to understand that the dance is a sign and symbol of spiritual victory. An example is taken from the Prophetess Miriam after the people of Israel's victory at the "Reed Sea," a narrative privileged and precious to the African American experience. The dance is also employed when one has a request before the Lord. It can be interpreted as a sign that one believes God will fulfill the request or make another way possible in anticipated victory. Or one might dance in the midst of one's storm, dancing to express a faith that God will bring deliverance. Often the Saints danced just after the sermon to affirm their confidence in the preached word. This was often the case at New Hope.

Dr. Clark was a profound preacher, and after having illuminated the textual meaning and providing an appropriate application and demonstration of the hand of God in our midst, he would move into the "whoop," a melding of words and melody. The preacher identifies his most comfortable musical key and scale, a key that fits his vocal range, saving the higher notes for the greater emphasis. All "whoops" are sung in a minor key, creating a sound reminiscent of African American Spirituals. As the preacher concludes his message, he moves into a melodic-verbal riff akin to jazz improvisation. A skillful whooper will reinforce the primary theme of the word he has preached, accentuating the message in a heart-felt manner. One has to have a good singing voice to be a good whooper. A good whooper will bring the church gathering to their feet and since they are already on their feet, they might as well dance. And they do.

■ ■ ■

I knew intuitively that the relationship with Richard could not be replicated. I gave no energy to trying to find another male lover. During my senior year at Norview, I dated three very nice young women; Jayne, Phyllis, and Valarie.

Phyllis and Valarie, I met at New Hope. Jayne and her family were friends to the Wells family as they rented the "A" Avenue homestead when we moved to Coronado. There was always this unspoken sense that Jayne and I would at some point date one another and bring the families closer. However, that's not quite how things evolved.

Phyllis was the pastor's daughter. She also sang in the youth choir. During my brief tenure as chief musician, I appointed her as choir director. We worked closely together, identifying songs and learning the choral parts. Gradually, we became affectionate. We were both trying to live a "holy life," so sex was never discussed, though we had some steamy arousal sessions at the base of the stairwell trying to say good night. Bernie Boo liked Phyllis and, with little provocation, invited she and her parents over for a Sunday dinner.

It was Valarie who would educate me on heterosexuality. Shortly after we met, Valarie shared a personal dilemma that she was facing. She did not want to still be a virgin when she turned 17, which would occur in the next six months. Her dilemma was how to find the "right guy." After a few discussions, we made a pact to work together to identify the "right guy" for her first sexual encounter. We played this game for several months, never quite identifying "Mr. Right." Confession: I didn't look that hard, for all the apparent reasons. I just figured if I could eliminate all the competition, I would be the only man left standing.

My approach worked, for a little while. Unfortunately, I knew very little about the female body and actually very little about my own. Valarie was a very beautiful Black woman; honey brown, shapely, with beautiful full breasts, and a great deal of sexual freedom. She was one of seven daughters and her mother had provided her with significant insight regarding the sexual encounter.

Valarie understood arousal and she knew that she was supposed to experience orgasm. I had heard in some "guy talk" that females could "cum" as well, but I knew nothing about the ins and outs of that process. Valarie's mother tried to help me when I made a comment that it takes longer for women to be aroused and ready for sex than a man.

She objected and suggested that "every woman has a certain spot, and it's the responsibility of her man to know that spot, because all he has to do is touch that spot and she will be ready."

This open mother of seven knew something!

Valarie would meet another young man before the year was out; a more sexually informed young man, who outperformed me. She would share bits and pieces of their sexual encounters.

Statements like, "He's not quick to 'cum' like you," and "he stays hard a long time and gives me time to enjoy myself."

Secretly, I was envious and wanted to be a fly on the wall to view their performance. Obviously, it was not to be.

There was a school-wide talent show in the spring of my senior year. I auditioned and made the show, although I felt an uncertain palpitation about the whole endeavor. The song I sang was "Rock a Bye Your Baby with a Dixie

Melody." I knew there was something not quite right about the song and my singing of it, but I couldn't put my finger on the problem. I was dating Jayne by this time, and she looked up to me as her boyfriend and was proud that I had made the cut. She came to one of the rehearsals and when I sang that lower register of the lyric "a million baby kisses I'll deliver," she screamed out loud and I was convinced to proceed. But, there remained a still small voice hinting that something about that "opportunity" was also not quite right.

4

You come all the way with me...don't leave me now.
—Traditional

In early September of 1968, Bernie Boo and I stood in line at the Bursar's office of Virginia Union University in Richmond, Virginia, with that $500 whole-life insurance policy she had taken out when I was five. Tuition for my freshman year was $1500. Fortunately, I was awarded a small scholarship and a student loan to cover the remaining balance.

With this accomplished, we headed toward Kingsley Hall, the freshman dorm. In the Bursar's office line, I had met Tally, my first roommate. He was a native New Yorker, short in stature, about 5'6", and muscular with a wrestler's build. He had dark skin like a deep rich chocolate with beautiful, straight white teeth which shone brightly when he smiled. He wore a neatly round-shaped tapered-back afro; a primary symbol of the times, Black is Beautiful! He was articulate, appeared easy-going, and neither one of us knew anyone else, so why not room together? Second major issue resolved. In a few weeks, I would meet Gussie, Ross, and Brother to form an emerging collective soon to be known on campus as "The Church Boys (Bois)"

Gussie was a native of Richmond, Virginia, so we operated in his backyard. Gussie was the shortest of the group, probably 5'2". Interestingly, he was the centering force in the group; very passive-aggressive and never a visible leader, always leading from the rear. What one learned to listen for were his concluding remarks.

He had a capacity for summation: "Lovely concert, but what is it about us that we just can't be on time?...We have to have an entrance!" Or, "That's not the right dress for her"..."I'm sorry, don't want to hurt nobody's feelings, ain't talking 'bout nobody's Momma, but Honey, you feel me."

Ross, a Pensacola, Florida native, had honey brown light skin and a moderate build. He was a man with an engaging smile, straight/curly dark brown hair, glistening eyes, and was a member of Jerusalem Holy Church where Bishop Annie B. Chamblin was pastor. Bishop Chamblin was also the denominational vice president of Mount Sinai Holy Church of America. The origin of our notoriety as the "Church Bois" may have come from the way Bishop honored us. Many Sunday mornings, we would be chauffeured to the church by her daughter and son-in-law, Elder Brown. Their stretch black Cadillac would pull into the parking lot just outside of our dorm where we would be anxiously waiting, dressed "to the T," and ready to pile into the back seats.

Given this repetitive sight, somebody on campus had to have asked the question, "Who are these Negros?"

Jerusalem Holy Church in Richmond is one of over 125 churches comprising the denomination of Mt. Sinai Holy Church of America. A part of its uniqueness is its founder, an African American woman, Ida B. Robinson, also a native of Pensacola, Florida. Bishop Robinson moved to Philadelphia in 1917, and upon concluding a ten-day fast in her small mission church, Bishop Robinson believed that she received two messages from the Holy Ghost; first, to come out on Mt. Sinai, and second, "I (God) will use you to loose the women."

True to her prophetic vision, the denomination has consistently been headed by women from 1924 to 2001.

Their doctrine includes a strict literal interpretation of the biblical texts affirming the trinity, conversion, repentance, salvation, and entire sancti- fication. It was their interpretation and application of "entire sanctification" which presented some ideological difficulties, at least from my perspective.

Men and women's bodies were to be fully clothed at all times. Yet, cloth- ing regulations for the women were stricter than for the men, as the hem of their dresses were always to be below their knees. Women were forbidden to wear sheer stockings, nor should they wear pants. The only colors women were to wear were the modest colors of black, brown, blue, and white. Jewelry was also forbidden, including wedding rings. A married woman could have a wedding ring, but the ring was to be attached to a pendant that could be worn near the left shoulder of their garments.

If it was reported that if a member's conduct was outside of "entire sanc- tification," there was a policy of confrontation. That's what happened to me, even though I was never a member of the church.

In the second semester of my freshman year, I joined the college thespians as one of the characters in a politically radical play entitled "Black Out." It's important to remember that 1968-1969 were years of tremendous social and political unrest and acrimony. Robert F. Kennedy and Dr. Martin Luther King, Jr. had been assassinated, the Vietnam War was being openly protested in the streets, Black people had rioted in many of the larger metropolises, and Black is Beautiful, coupled with an arresting New Black Consciousness, were all in the mix. In this same time frame, Queer people, led by Marsha P. Johnson, a mature Black trans woman, initiated Stonewall.

"Black Out" sought to speak to the changing consciousness of the time, with an emphasis on the emerging Black Pride Movement and the open ac- knowledgment and celebration of Black contributions to the world. The play contained a modicum of profanity; a few words like damn, hell, and maybe shit. Theater had not progressed to the "f" word. Nevertheless, word got back to Bishop Chamblin that I was in the play, and that I was using profanity. She confronted me.

Bishop Chamblin possessed an imposing physique. As I remember, she was about six-feet-tall, full-chested, and weighed a minimum of 250 pounds. She had a dark almond complexion with penetrating dark brown eyes, which felt like she was looking right through you. And she was.

To confront me, she invited me to her home, which was walking distance from the campus. She was busy cooking the evening meal for her husband when I arrived. She explained that she was not just a pastor and bishop, but also a wife. When she had the cooking well underway, she came into the living room where I was seated and began to explain her concern. She let me know, beyond the shadow of a doubt, that my cursing, even in a make-believe circumstance, was ungodly. It was not the behavior of an entirely sanctified man and I should drop out of the play, lest I lose my influence as a Christian.

I thanked her for her concern, we breathed a word of prayer, and I left. Now that I think about it, she may have been recruiting me for membership. As I recall, Elder Brown invited me to preach at one of their mid-week services, and was mildly impressed with my sermonic style.

At this juncture, the play only had a few more weekends to run, and I wasn't about to destabilize our ensemble and lose my credibility with the thespians. I wasn't a member of her church, so I rode out the storm and the issue passed.

What Bishop did not know was that the play was scheduled to be presented again at one of our tri-college affiliates, Concordia College in Moorhead, Minnesota in the fall semester of 1969. I wasn't about to miss this free trip to Minnesota, even if it was scheduled in their winter; a season I knew nothing about. While Black/Queerness is innately a risk, one should not allow one's status to preclude all risk-taking.

I guess Bishop felt like I was one of her own, even if I had not formally joined her church. She provided me with weekly transportation to and from worship, even though worship was an all-day experience. There was the sweet, floating morning ride to the church in the stretch Cadillac, and there was generally exuberant worship beginning at 11 a.m., running indefinitely.

After morning worship, there was a break, providing time to read some portion of our course requirements. But before too long, there would be a call to the dinner table. There is very little about those dinners that I remember. I'm sure they were primary to average fare, but the piece de resistance each Sunday was the homemade yeast rolls; served piping hot, golden brown on the outside, crusty overall, flaky, yet moist on the inside. Dough that had been allowed to fully rise to the height of fluffiness. Manna from on High! If Israel's Manna tasted like these rolls, Israel would have not complained.

"Feed me 'til I want no more! Glory!"

Evening service began at seven p.m. This evening worship service was a more spiritual encounter. Fewer visitors attended the evening service, so in some ways, the worship had a "just family" disposition. Prophecy was a prominent "Gift of the Spirit" operating at Jerusalem Holy Church, and there were two acknowledged prophets among the laypersons, Sister Rivers and Brother Frank. Sister Rivers was the most respected of the two. Her features were similar to Bishop Chamblin; tall, 200 pounds, with a black walnut skin tone. But, her unique distinction was an inch-and-a-half streak of pure white hair which began just above her forehead, running to the base of her neck. This marking among African Americans is respected as an indication of some divine anointing and/or spiritual calling. The anticipation that the prophets might "speak a prophetic word" for church/family members was a draw to the evening service.

Sister Rivers was not only the most respected, she was also the most feared. A prophecy could come forward at any time during worship.

Without notice, Sister Rivers would rise from her seat in high drama and begin to walk the aisles chanting, "Jesus, Jesus, Jesus!"

The Saints would begin to chant with her. The fearful members would cower in their seats, hoping that she would not come to them. I have seen members begin to weep frantically as she approached them to make her prophetic pronouncement. Most often, the pronouncement was a corrective of some kind. The member to which this was addressed would be brought by the hand from their seat to the altar for prayer and be accused of living a "less than entirely sanctified" lifestyle. The attention of all worshipers would now be focused on this individual until they repented, arose from their knees, and began to victoriously "dance a holy dance before the Lord."

Now, I would be less than authentic if I did not point out that sometimes Sister Rivers got the message wrong. Like the time when this young couple, both raised in the church, fell in love and married. They had only been married a few weeks and the bride was so proud of her wedding pin and her handsome husband.

In an evening service, Sister Rivers rose from her seat chanting "Jesus, Jesus, Jesus," went over to the new bride, and prophesied that her new husband would die!

Needless to say, this terrified the entire church body. As I recall, Bishop Chamblin followed up with a teaching regarding prophecy which sought to draw a distinction between physical and spiritual death. Bishop explained that Sister Rivers' true message was that the new groom was approaching spiritual death. Religious spiritual prowess sometimes runs amok.

There was also the time Sister Rivers repeatedly accused a single young woman of promiscuity. The young woman in question went along with being brought to the altar, but was furious about being called out publicly for something she did not do. Her mother was a long-standing member of the church and she felt powerless to confront the spiritual authority of Sister Rivers and Bishop Chamblin. The mother and daughter met with Bishop privately during that same week and resolved the issue. As might be predicted, when the young woman came of age, she, along with many others, left the church.

That spring, Virginia Union's Concert Choir had their Spring Tour '69. Our director, Dr. Odell Hobbs, unknown to me and probably most of the choral members, founded the music department at Union and curated a curriculum establishing a major in music education. Dr. Hobbs was slight in stature, probably under 5'4", and was losing his natural hair. He wore a toupee and, on certain occasions, a full wig. He dressed with style, though his pants always seemed to display his bulge. He was a gay man, but given his position, he was wise to be on the down-low. Dr. Hobbs was a genius.

Where to start... It is said in community that he was born with undeveloped fingers. As I recall, he had a thumb and first two index fingers on his right hand, and just a thumb and first index finger on his left. Where there are generally other fingers, he had nubs. Dr. Hobbs was a classical pianist. By his own admission, he survived college by playing piano for gospel choirs and Black Churches. There was no music or genres you could put in front of him that he could not play. He had a greater love for voice, so he gave it much consideration and trained his ear to clarity, textures, timbre, and tenors of the human voice.

When we got to New York, we arrived the night before the concert, with rehearsal scheduled for the next morning. We would be singing under Carnegie's music conductor. He was European, with a thick accent. I don't remember much else about him, except that he was astounded at our sound and he told us openly. One could tell on his face he had questioned what the nuance of the Black voice would do to "Hayden's Mass in D Minor." He was pleasantly surprised.

Hayden's Mass opens with "Kyrie Eleison," interpreted from the Greeks - "Lord have mercy," and from the Hebrews - "Comfort me, soothe me, show me your steadfast love."

If I were to put on my preaching cap right now, I'd have to say, "Come on Mr. Hayden...what you gonna tell us Black folk about God's mercy...Sing on! What you gonna tell us, Mr. Hayden, about God's comfort and presence?"

We have had Deacon's knee bowed and body bent for generations who opened their prayers pleading to God chanting, "Lord have mercy...Lord have mercy...Lord have mercy for mercy... suits our case. What's that you say, Mr. Hayden? Amen."

Dr. Hobbs created an unsurpassed network of alumni and pastors, graduates of the Virginia Union Seminary, up and down the East coast, from New York to Atlanta. Between the two networks, the concert choir would perform to substantive crowds almost nightly for a solid week. It was quite an experience. I have no details on how the money was distributed, but I believe the concerts were a communal and economic win-win.

So, my second great adventure, thanks to Virginia Union, came in the fall of my sophomore year when as aforementioned, I was off to Concordia College to once again present the play, "Black Out." The thespians of Virginia Union had been invited to present the play in the fall semester of 1969 as part of a government-funded endeavor entitled "The Exchange Program." Its purpose was to increase the enrollment of Black students at this predominantly white institution. An understanding of the implications of this decision can only fully be achieved with some understanding of the context of the 1960s.

The eternal flame that was Kennedy and the dream of Dr. King had both been extinguished. Black militancy and a new Black consciousness constituted the milieu of the time. Stokely Carmichael, Angela Davis, and the Black Panthers were some of the prominent architects of the Black Power Movement, while Black musicians were also off the charts. James Brown seemed to release a new song every other week.

He reinforced the theme of the time, "Say it Loud, I'm Black and I'm proud," even as he kept us "On the Good Foot." While Aretha testified, "I Never Loved a Man the Way I Love You," Marvin Gaye recommended "Sexual Healing," even as he raised the question, "What's Going On?" Stevie Wonder answered him back, "Very Superstitious."

Once the departure date was set, I called Bernie Boo to discuss the matter with her and made my request for a new pair of boots because of the late fall Minnesota snow. She sent me the money and I promptly proceeded to downtown Richmond and bought a pair of brown, above the ankle Florsheim boots with black leather soles. When we got off the bus in Moorhead, I was confident that I was prepared for this endeavor, even as I literally slid into the experiential theater where the play would be performed for the rest of the campus. I had boots, but not the right boots for Minnesota snow and ice. This was lesson number one.

I first learned about Race eavesdropping on a conversation between my mother and father when I was around six or seven years old. We were sitting in the kitchen at the home in Coronado at the table which was hinged like a Murphy bed, though we seldom put it up against the wall unless we were washing the kitchen floor. What was unusual about this conversation was that Daddy was leading it and he was telling Momma about an incident that occurred on his job at the post office between a worker and a supervisor.

What struck me as odd about the conversation was that as Daddy would describe the men, Momma would periodically interrupt Daddy and ask, "Is he a one or a two?"

I tried to be patient as long as I could, but I finally interrupted and asked, "What's a one and what's a two?"

Daddy said, "White people are ones, and you and I and your Momma are twos."

I immediately objected saying, "No, I'm a one, not a two."

Momma and Daddy looked at each other with that look that says, 'He will come to understand, or we are headed for some real difficulties with this child.'

Whiteness as a dominating cultural norm is pervasive in the United States. It's in the educational process via the stories that are told and untold. The Tulsa Massacre as an example. But, the brand of whiteness produced, nurtured, reinforced, and protected at Concordia College, etched in Lutheranism, is a special experience for Black people. The college was established to preserve Nordic culture.

Du Bois posed the question, "How does it feel to be a problem?"

I pose the question, "How does it feel to be an experiment?"

The play was received as well as might be expected with very few questions raised in the talk-back sessions after its conclusion. Perhaps, because on campus, whiteness demands that we always be polite, never raising our voices. Perhaps for the audience there was difficulty in framing questions for fear of being impolite. Nevertheless, in the back of my mind, this was an opportunity for me to learn to deal with white people. For, if I could survive in this 99 percent white environment, I believed I could survive anywhere. I accepted the challenge to become part of the experiment of exchange and returned to the campus the next semester in January of 1970.

It was not easy to leave my guys, the Church Bois, having shared much of ourselves with each other and having created a nice interactive flow. They of course prophesied to me, though their concerns were not mine.

One of them said, "Suppose you fall in love with some white girl, and we never see you again?"

Others just said they didn't have a "good feeling" about the move. What was a feeling of fear and dread for them was a spirit of adventure for me. Yet, there was some truth in their prophetic expressions. I would conceive a child with Gwen during spring break of that first semester and we would marry in May; a short-lived marriage of less than two years.

It would be many years before I would see the Church Bois again. Brother would pass away from a disease that strongly resembled HIV/AIDS. The other two would marry, have children, and divorce. One would even come out as gay and leave his ministry. And they were correct that this experiment would serve as a major trajectory for the balance of my lived experience, including the future white wife.

One of the contradictory policies of The Exchange Program was a guideline which prevented an exchange student from transferring to the visiting college for one year after their visiting semester. So, I returned as a full-fledged "Concordia Cobber" the summer of 1971.

Not much had changed. At that point, what used to be a Black student room, which was now a Black student house, was just across from campus. The big fun of the week was the dance that would be held on Friday and/or Saturday night. We treated it like church, dressed up and cologned down.

I had a few favorite outfits I would wear to the dance or on special occasions. I traded those Florsheim slick-bottomed leather boots for a pair of knee-high tan lace up rubber-soled boots. I considered them my dress shoes and wore them with everything. One outfit was a black, wool knit, one-piece jump suit with the collar trimmed in baby blue. It zipped from the crotch to the neckline with its own zipper shield of the same material. Or, I might wear my lilac-colored, white pinstriped gaucho pants and vest, with a long-sleeved button-down cream shirt that had a wide pointed collar.

Though seldom intentionally coordinated, we would often trade off with the Black students at Minnesota State University in Moorhead, which was within walking distance, windchill permitting.

When they would let me, on Friday nights, I would hang with the five Black men who originated from the West Side of Chicago. They were members of a Lutheran church on the West Side and had been recruited by Concordia. They referred to themselves as "The Dead Soldiers." According to them, "Dead Soldier" status could not be bestowed, but could only be achieved.

To be a "Dead Soldier," one must drink a full bottle of Boone's Farm Strawberry Hill wine and smoke two joints, by oneself. I was an unofficial "Dead Soldier" who would drop by their suite of rooms after dinner around 6 p.m. and see if I could try out one more time. From there, we would make a joint entrance into the Black house and give new energy to the party!

When the dance got really good to us, we would yell out, "Party over here!"

The goal, after all, was to make some connection with a female which might lead to Marvin's recommendation of "Sexual Healing. "

Given the regularity of these Friday and Saturday nights, we acquired at least a passing knowledge of most of the students and we could spot a visitor. After a few months, I noticed this brother who would show up at the dance periodically, suited down, and upon closer examination, I found out he also drove a late-model vehicle. I wondered what he did and where he worked.

At some point, I introduced myself and made small talk. He worked for a company, Cargill, that I had never heard of. He was a salt salesman. Who sold salt? Moorhead was on his sales route, and being intuitive, he knew that Black college students partied on Friday and Saturday nights, so on those weeks when he was near or in town, he would stop into the dance. He suggested that I consider working for Cargill, once I had my degree in hand. I thought it was a great lead and tucked away the information.

Some of the Black women made friends with the white women in their dorms. After watching these Black women dress and go to the dance on Friday nights, some of the white women inquired if they might attend – I was not finding any of them attractive. However, one Friday night, Linda, a Sister, introduced me to one of her white friends, Lydia, whom she said wanted to meet me. Lydia was beautiful; a little plump, a great smile that lit up the room, a magnetic personality, a fabulous sense of humor - and she was interested in meeting me?!

I had a very uneasy feeling about this encounter, as I was quite proud of the positions I held within the Black Student Union, Harambee Wiese, choir director for our ensemble, and a member of the board. To seriously date a white woman was considered sleeping with the enemy. However, if I was uncertain about what I wanted, Lydia was not.

Lydia dressed in a very sophisticated style. She would wear jeans and a sweater on many occasions, but when she came to the dance, she would wear some sophisticated tailored dress that looked like it came out of the Oval Room at Dayton's in Minneapolis. One dress was white with red roses scattered throughout the fabric. The chest area was slightly open and it was belted, with an ankle-length hem. She was not confused and was not trying to look like the other Black women. She was clearly her own person and had her own style. Other brothers might ask her to dance from time to time, but she would let them know they were knocking on the wrong door. She knew what, and who, she wanted.

At some point after our relationship developed, she contracted a case of mono. After having been apart several weeks, I asked if it would be okay for me to come and visit her at her home in North Dakota. I'm not sure quite how I accomplished this, but somehow, I made it to the farm. I wore my knee-high boots and purple striped knickers. Her mother looked out of the window as I got out of the vehicle. She began to laugh, and could hardly compose herself, but Norwegian social culture demands politeness. I think Lydia's father shortened his day to come in from the barn to meet this Black man his oldest child was interested in.

The encounter was polite and there was no real chill in the air. What they wanted to know was my intention regarding employment after graduation. I told them I planned to go to the Cities and get a job with Cargill. They laughed, not in my face, but no doubt after I left. They were agricultural people and understood the vastness of Cargill. From their perspective, I was a "city boy." What could I possibly offer Cargill that would warrant my being hired? But, they were willing to play the game and see.

I graduated from Concordia College in the spring of 1973. Needless to say, Bernie Boo and Leon made the trip from Norfolk. Momma wore a navy blue suit and matching large pill-box veiled hat. Daddy was attired in a regular brown business suit. He looked really nice, except he was "drunk as a skunk." After the conclusion of the graduation service, Boo, Daddy and I were standing outside of the auditorium, talking with each other.

Momma said, "I would like to meet some of your professors."

I immediately began to scope the crowd, identified my professors, and made introductions. Bernie Boo was something else.

While Lydia was very present during their brief visit, I don't remember her parents being there. We were not engaged, so there was no reason for them to attend. To their absolute amazement, as prophesied, I went down to the Cities that summer and got a job with Cargill. I know this created a significant change in their opinion of me. What I never understood, however, was the Cargill job was my primary link to acceptance in the family. They were soybean farmers.

5

When I Rose this Morning...I said Thank you Lord.
—Traditional

To my great joy, Bernie Boo and Leon safely got on the plane back to Norfolk. The week after graduation, I did just what Dwayne Merriweather told me to do. I went downtown Minneapolis, found the building that housed Cargill's Human Resources Department, and made an appointment for an interview. It turned out to be one of those fortuitous encounters. The gentleman I interviewed with, Dave May, had also been a manager in the Salt Department. He knew Dwayne, so he reasoned if I knew Dwayne and he knew Dwayne, I was probably a good Black person.

At the very least, Dwayne was a resource to verify my viability as a candidate. It did not occur to me that I was one of the first groups of Blacks aggressively hired into the company. I had missed that indicator. In a matter of days, the letter came offering me the opportunity to be employed by the largest privately-held corporation in the world.

The 1970's was clearly a period when white institutions, in their concerted effort to hire significant numbers of Black people, developed "Programs." I was leaving Concordia's "Exchange Program" to now enter Cargill's "Intern Program." However, there was a significant difference in the two approaches.

I felt Concordia College was a taker, open to receive all that students of color brought to their campus, especially the federal money. In contrast, Cargill's Intern Program provided plush experiences, testing the individual's preparedness to enter their unique agricultural workforce, marshaled by the cultural milieu of the one percent.

The Intern Program was a five-week excursion, designed to provide an overview of the vastness of the company. The other Black person in my cohort was a woman named Sharon. She was a graduate of a Historical Black College or University (HBCU), who visibly, was in over her head. Our cohort would party together on the weekends, sharing what we had gleaned from our outings. She was clearly frightened.

After a drink or two, Sharon would confide in me, "I don't know how you do it. How do you just talk with them and you appear so comfortable? I don't know if I can do this."

The corporate milieu was palpable.

Each week, interns were flown to various Cargill operations, housed in the finest hotels of that city with expense accounts for meals and transportation, and receipts not needed. The objective was to gain insight into that particular business. Among the trips I remember were visiting Chicago to see the Grain Division and Board of Trade; New Orleans to see the Transportation Department; Sioux City, Iowa to see the Soybean Association; Rockford, Illinois to see the Chemical Department; and a week with Dwayne on his Salt Department route in Minnesota. Near the conclusion of these experiences, we returned to Human Resources and were queried to identify the business that impressed us the most and to choose the department in which we would like to work.

In that final week, at the cohort gathering, Sharon asked me to stand beside her as she called her mother to say she had been fired. With tears streaming, snot flowing, yet maintaining an insisting voice that she had given the opportunity her very best, she was broken to her core. Not easy to disappoint Black mothers, particularly with only six weeks on the job. It was long enough for her mother to brag about her milestone accomplishment, which she then had to go back and recant. Sharon had missed two Monday morning flights to her destinations.

I don't think that the inadequacy was in the HBCU itself, but I left the school for that very reason – to be able to survive in whiteness, especially in a white upper-class milieu; one that was not only palpable, but threatening. As a person of color, and particularly a Black person, our presence is proceeded by so many negative means that seek to define us. There is always a sense we are being measured in some way, and it is easy to believe we are being perceived as being "less than." These unarticulated expectations often stifle and silence us. One usually needs more than cocaine, weed, or alcohol to survive.

I found it interesting that Sharon asked me to stand with her at her moment of "wreckage," instead of my white roommate from New Orleans who she was sleeping with, and who was also a member of our cohort. I guess it just "bees" that way sometimes.

I think I threw Dave May a curve ball when I selected the Soybean Association. His face twitched in surprise. Nevertheless, he still set up an interview with the divisional head, Don Leavenworth. The interview would be at corporate headquarters, a French Chateau built in 1931, with 410 feet of access to Gray Bay of Lake Minnetonka, conversationally referred to as the "Lake Office." Divisional heads had their offices on the first floor. Corporate officers, the president, vice president, and other administration had offices on the second, accessible by a curved marble staircase or the elevator.

Rufus Rand of Minneapolis Gas Company built the Lake Office in the middle of the Great Depression for a cost of $400,000. It was purchased by the Cargill family in 1944 and contained 63 rooms; 14 bedrooms, 16 bathrooms, along with 13 fireplaces. The finest woods - oak, walnut, mahogany - splashed the interior walls, doors, and moldings. The outer brick walls were 17 inches thick.

The Chateau itself sat back almost a mile from the frontage road along Highway 55. At the time of its construction, the swimming pool was the largest private pool in North America, boasting a capacity of 1.3 million gallons.

I rented a car and drove out to the Chateau the morning of my interview. Upon entering, I was greeted by a very attractive middle-aged white woman who was the receptionist. I announced that I had a meeting with Mr. Leavenworth. She made a brief call to his administrator and I was ushered back to his "fishbowl" office, large enough to seat ten people if needed. His desk was positioned toward the middle of the room, with several tall windows to his back and glass to the ceiling in front of him, complimented by cherry wood halfway up the wall.

After the politeness and preliminary introductions, the conversation turned to the more pertinent question, "What attracts you to the Soybean Association?"

With a fair degree of excitement, I detailed three major factors. First, the idea of production; that from a single bean, three different products are extracted; meal, oil and hulls. Processed from every 60-pound bushel of beans, there is 48 pounds of meal, 10.5 pounds of oil, and 1.5 pounds of hulls. But, what I found even more interesting was the concept of a crushing margin. When the potential revenues are posted against the cost of the beans, a margin of profit is derived. From this margin, one subtracts the cost of production and the remainder is the projected profit. What I did not know at the time was that I was talking directly to Mr. Leavenworth in his language that he prized, and I was also telling his story.

What I would later learn is at the time of my interview, Leavenworth was new to his job. Another major factor, greatly impacting the context, was that prices in the Soybean Association were at an all-time high. A decade before, in 1960, the average cost of soybeans was $2.50 per bushel. At the time of my interview, soybeans were at a record high of $12.00 per bushel. The business was hot and crushing margins were wide.

The story is told that Leavenworth got his promotion after a stellar performance in the previous year as an account manager at an export location. He was the first to predict that crushing margins would go to a dollar per bushel, and through some political shenanigans, he wrapped up his entire yearly production at a crushing margin of one dollar or more. When one considers that an average plant can process 50,000 bushels a day, with a cost of 30 cents a bushel, this could generate somewhere between 12 and 13 million dollars of profit for the year.

As they say in the trade, "Not a bad lick!"

When I returned to the Human Resources Department, I was offered a position of junior merchant in the Soybean Association. My first location assignment was in Chicago. I called Blanche almost immediately to tell her I had gotten the job in Chicago and asked if could I stay with them until Lydia and I were married the following year. We negotiated a monthly stipend and my arrival into Chicago was paved with an easy landing.

Needless to say, I was more than delighted to catch a metropolitan assignment in an agricultural business. Lydia was more than delighted as well, and her folks were utterly astounded. How could this Black, purple gaucho-wearing guy do this? A city man with no agricultural background obtained a job at the largest privately held corporation in the world and landed a first assignment in Chicago.

They were just unfamiliar with the power of "Programs."

Lydia and I had agreed that once she had finished her senior year at Concordia, we would marry shortly after her graduation. This gave me an opportunity to work for the year to save the vast amount of money for the ring, the wedding, the honeymoon, and the new apartment. We would get engaged somewhere along the way, after I had paid for her ring - a three-quarter carat marquise cut set in white gold. I would wear a white gold wedding band. I didn't need diamonds as Lydia had already given me a multi-faceted diamond ring set in yellow gold for my graduation. I was on the hook!

Aunt Blanche and Uncle Boe had changed residence since I was last in Chicago. They now lived in a beautiful, brick single-family home off of 79th and Paxton. The front entrance foyer was small, but with a powder room immediately to the left. The stairs to the second floor were straight ahead against the left wall with a closet underneath. To the right, there was one step down into a sizable living room which flowed left into the dining room just off the kitchen, further to the left. The three bedrooms were all upstairs. It was a beautiful home. Blanche had already changed the colors in the kitchen to yellow, her favorite color.

I find it hard to believe, to this day, that in the course of one full year, in the metropolis of Chicago, I did not meet one other woman of interest. I met a couple of men, but nothing to take home to Momma. I did have a couple of acquaintances at the office who provided a few intimate encounters; the guy who distributed the mail and one of the secretaries in the Grain Division.

I didn't return to Ebeneezer Baptist, as I wanted a little distance between the Lee's and myself. After all, I was now a grown man with a great job, about to be engaged, and on the cusp of creating my own life. I joined a smaller Baptist church in the community, within walking distance. I think Richard had played there at some point and the church may have been his recommendation. I didn't like the experience, no move of the Spirit, no drum, and the minister's preaching left a significant portion to be desired.

I would come back to the house every Sunday afternoon and complain about his preaching, and Blanche would say, "Maybe he's not the right pastor for you."

I think she was hoping I would move on so that my conversations at Sunday dinner might change.

About six months in, the guy who was my senior merchant got transferred. The incoming senior merchant, also named Dave, had this same position for what might be described as an inordinate number of years. Most of those years were spent at the plant in Wichita, Kansas. Dave was a smart white man without family name or pedigree. He saw me as a "nigger" and while he was careful and polite, he did think that we were not in the same lane. One Friday after work, we found ourselves at a bar where a pianist was the primary entertainment. As we stood around the piano, drinks nearby, I put some money in the vase and requested she play the song, "Them There Eyes."

His face lit up with surprise and his mouth flew open to say, "That's pretty classy!"

I just smiled as I thought to myself, 'Well, who did you think I was?'

However, Dave's central focus from day one was to understand why he had been overlooked for so long, and whether or not this move to Chicago would lead to his becoming an account manager. Either way, taking the transfer to Chicago, the center of agricultural business, was a good lick. The head offices of most of our competitors were either just around the corner or just across the street. Opportunity was everywhere. He came in one morning, shaking hands all around the office, and announced that he had taken a significant management position with a competitor and he had just come in to clear his desk.

He said to me, "Maybe my leaving will be good for you."

Dave turned out to be prophetic. His position was not filled and I became a full merchant, on trial.

I had a great boss in Chicago by the name of Tom Morrow. Tom's management style with me was to be the "big brother." It worked for me. This meant that we could say almost anything to each other, but words spoken should be evaluated relative to tone, distinguishing that which is humor from that which is serious. We had excellent communication.

Tom's primary preoccupation was a family issue - his wife Gini. As I recall, there were at least two children and thoughts of a third. It's important to remember that the 1970s was a season where the drug of choice for suburban housewives was Valium. It seemed nearly every Cargill married man's wife was on Valium, including Gini. From a distance, it seemed she was not experiencing the tranquility she was anticipating. Many were the evenings where Tom raced out of the office, stuffing papers into his briefcase, trying to catch the early train to the suburbs after a phone call from Gini.

My future wife was finishing her degree and not on Valium. Yet in time, she would become a focal point for the wives at corporate gatherings. Lydia would also become a focal point for some of the men in the Chicago office of Cargill.

Many seemed to marvel, "Why would Lydia, a tall, beautiful, highly intelligent white woman marry a Black man without name or pedigree, when clearly, she could have any man she wanted?"

And Lydia was charming - she could charm the pants off of all the men in the room, even as she played "girlfriend" to the women. External physical attraction, coupled with high intelligence, perception, and drive produced a riveting force.

Our office was on LaSalle Street, just around the corner from the Chicago

Board of Trade, what traders refer to as the futures market. For me, futures trading was part of the fascination of the business. There are many ways to achieve the crushing margin, in cash commodities or in futures, or some combination or percentages of the two.

The office was leased by the Grain Division, but it housed several Cargill entities. In addition to the desks of nine to ten Grain Division merchants, there were six desks for the Soybean Complex. In the middle of the two groups of desks were two men who managed futures trading for our division. All futures trading orders, from all the plants, went through their hands, including the trading orders of upper management.

One day, our junior futures trader got sick and they needed someone to answer the phone, take the orders, and report the sales and purchases for the division. I was recruited, and of course, I was excited.

I did not know at the time the scuttlebutt that was brewing among the traders in the Grain Division. Apparently, one of their primary future traders, a non-degreed white boy from Skokie, thought that bringing me to the floor to answer the calls, report, and tally the trades was not a good idea.

Grain Division booths were on the opposite side of the trading pits, but every now and then I could see this gentleman eyeing me. I ignored it at first and re-focused on trades. At the end of the day, millions of soybean futures, thousands of tons of soy meal, and soy oil futures were successfully traded division-wide with only one error. Once trading ceased, the white boy from Skokie came across the pit to point out the single error.

As he was walking away, he said, "I told them you were gonna fuck it up!"

Once our side closed down for the trading day, I was taken to lunch at the Men's Club where we dined on lamb chops and turtle soup seasoned with sherry. When I got back to the office, the word on my performance had gotten around, and there were only accolades, signaling to me that there were lots of people watching. One of the primary and pervasive fears undergirding racial discrimination is Black Excellence.

The first year at Cargill in Chicago went very well. Lydia came to visit me twice. The first visit was a lot of "I've missed you so much." The second visit was to formalize our engagement.

On the initial visit, Blanche would not allow Lydia to stay in the house with us because she and I were not formally engaged. I found a half-decent hotel further down 79th Street. It was not in the best part of town, but was within walking distance of the house. I booked a room for the weekend. A day or two later, I had a premonition about finding a gun on the top shelf of the closet in the hotel room we had booked. I didn't let it bother me, but I kept it in my mind.

When Lydia arrived and we checked into the room and hung up our clothes for the weekend, I remembered the premonition. I walked over to the closet and checked the top shelf, and there it was - a huge pistol, the caliber of which was much greater than a .45. The question in my mind was how to get the gun to the front desk without appearing to be a robber, and to make sure my fingerprints were not on it. Praise Baby Jesus, we cautiously got that accomplished.

Lydia's second visit was a true celebration. I got on one knee and proposed, whipping out the marquise diamond ring. After she said "Yes," we went downtown to the restaurant with the "spinning silver salad bowl" and had a scrumptious meal. Lydia stayed with us at the house on this visit and the atmosphere for that weekend had a more familial texture, rich and sweet.

Later that week, when Blanche and I were alone, she commented to me almost in passing, "I should have thanked Lydia before she left, 'cause I got rolled over in the hay two nights, back-to-back. Something about having that white girl downstairs in your uncle's house raised his temperature."

We both let out belly laughs. Aunt Blanche was too much!

Lydia and I married in a small Methodist church in Warren, North Dakota. Needless to say, Boo was there, dressed in a flowing blue and white floor-length gown, with a smile so bright, you could not miss the pride. I think Momma asked Blanche to come be with her at the wedding, so she would not feel so isolated being the only Black woman at the gathering. Blanche also wore a modest blue floor-length gown. It met the requirements, but was without statement.

Well, maybe that's not true. It could be understood to say it was frugal.

That was an outstanding characteristic of Blanche's wardrobe. She never spent very much money on her clothing, even when her immediate social network all but demanded it. Ebeneezer Baptist was a class church; culturally Black, capitalist, patriarchal, and hetero-normative to its core.

It was the custom and expectation of the financial elites to give their wives mink coats on their 25th wedding anniversary. My recollection is that the assistant pastor and his wife had recently reached their 25th year mark as well. Now...how do I say this...her minks not only had that shimmer and glisten of fine furs, but also seemed to dance whenever she moved, even if it was just a quiver. And Lordie, don't let her walk down that center aisle with it on.

"Sweet Jesus how wonderful you are, you are the fairest of ten thousand to my soul!"

Glory!

No doubt Blanche's friends outside of the church, being familiar with the expectations of a Chicago class church, were also awaiting the unveiling of her mink. I think knowing Uncle Boe, he sent her downtown to the furrier and told her to pick out what she wanted.

Well...how do I describe this...Blanche's minks were milder, flatter minks. The individual furs also appeared to be almost matted, more like a blanket. It was clear that the furs were mink, but barely. Nevertheless, we all made much to-do about, gushed over, heaped praise on, and raved about the coat, even though it was obviously a frugal choice.

Daddy was also at the wedding, wearing his tuxedo. That was one of the things that I admired about him – dress-wise, he was ready for any occasion. His tux was black with curved silky satin lapels. He was drunk as a skunk, but present and accounted for at his son's wedding. He too was proud. Daddy was nervous as hell, but full of great joy. This was the first meeting of the in-laws, and in the good Norwegian fashion, civility trumped all.

Lydia's mother, Mardy, was a very loving individual and extremely astute. A doctor – a surgeon - whose anxiety level was too high for her to practice. So, in their small town, she operated somewhere between a medical nurse and, in an emergency, a doctor/surgeon.

Mardy stood next to my father in the reception line, and when it was all said and done, and we could all take a breath, she said of my father to the wedding party, "Say what you will, but he clearly and accurately pronounced every name of every individual that I introduced to him - without a stutter!"

An astute observer may have caught the two early-on indicators which suggested this marriage had a potential for turbulence. These indicators surfaced at the wedding and on the honeymoon.

Prior to the commencement of the wedding ritual, I was standing with my groomsmen at the rear of the church. Last minute guests arriving were signing the wedding book, when in comes one of Lydia's friends and cohorts from college. When I say she was strikingly beautiful, I mean gorgeous - blond, 5'2", 120 pounds, with a face of a white angel. All I did was look, but my mother-in-law saw the look and quickly retreated to the front of the church. I think I heard a disparaging word.

The second indicator presented itself during our honeymoon. Lydia had booked us "a cabin up north" for a week. Cabins up North in North Dakota in May are cold, damp, moldy enclaves. There were ten of them in this complex, owned by Sven, and the necessary layering of clothing did not make the experience better. I know that this idea was Lydia's, 'cuz I'm a city boy and I don't like cold, and I don't like damp, and I don't like mold. Bottom line:

We came home early from our honeymoon.

Back in Chicago, everything was ready. I found an apartment for us on North Sheridan Drive, across the street from a Synagogue and a small kids' park, with access to the lake.

I'm not sure how I secured it because it was a popular area. Our apartment was near those high-rise condominiums that Bob Newhart supposedly lived in. It was also in walking distance of the "L" train.

Within a week, Lydia got a job as a buyer for Marshall Fields. Who could ask for anything more? Sweet honey in the Rock!

This was the beginning of our excursion as a family working for Cargill. We owned that identity, and with it came a geographical relocation every two years. We were two years in Chicago, two years in Sioux City, Iowa, where my first child was born, and then two years in Cedar Rapids.

But now, as we sat across from my mother's casket, Lydia and I had lived in Minneapolis for the past year and a half. Fate of all fates, sixteen months prior, I was promoted to the Oil Desk at the Chateau, the Lake Office; the hot seat that if successfully navigated, leads to that upper middle-management position of account manager. The eight-year goal so close – it was definitely in tasteable range.

In the midst of my grief, my concern was what I did not know. I didn't know company policy regarding deaths, and I was so psychologically distraught that it did not even occur to me to call and ask. But I did know this, the culture did not like absence.

I was in bad shape psychologically and I could barely feel my legs in front of me as I walked, but I wasn't aware of this either. It did not really break through into my consciousness until that morning when Aunt Louise, with a grimace on her face, tried to push the church door against me as I stood on the incline of the steps as we were processing into Mt. Olive Church to funeralize my mother.

6

If it hadn't been for Jesus...where would I be?
—Traditional

There was a sinister atmosphere in my mother and father's home that I had not experienced before, and it was more than just Bernie Boo's absence. Yet, in many ways, it was fully because of her absence. There was a counter narrative unfolding in front of my face, the essence of which scorched my brain. It triggered a flashback to my last visit with MomMatt in the hospital as she was dying.

Momma quietly led me to MomMatt's bedside. I was astounded by the number of tubes in her arms and taped into her nose. I had never seen anything quite like it. I had only spoken a few words to her and she signaled, by the wave of her hand, for me to leave. Momma said MomMatt didn't want me to see her in that condition. I received what Momma said, but it didn't sit well in my ten-year-old gut. There was just something about the way she waved me away. It felt like rejection.

When I visited Bernie Boo the week before her death, she laid out all of their business documentation which was kept in the safe. But there were also additional documents in the small filing cabinet in Daddy's closet. When I returned seven days later, some documents were missing. I initially thought that Momma had changed her mind and was directing me to those documents in Daddy's closet. I went there, and found that even more documents were missing.

■ ■ ■

Momma died the Saturday morning after Thanksgiving. I arrived in Norfolk the next day, but Blanche had beat me there, even on a holiday weekend. Louise, or Pooh as we called her, arrived on Monday. One of the oddities of this new context was the absence of any conversation in the house. In addition, there was an unarticulated, yet behavioral, diminishing of my role. Even though I was the son, their nephew, 29 years of age - they were in charge.

Granted, they were my aunts, but more importantly they were my father's sisters. Blanche appeared to be handling all the business matters on behalf of my father. For these two sisters, the appearance was their role to protect their brother, especially as he laid incoherent on the floor in an alcoholic stupor. Many years would pass before I questioned how he remained in a drunken stupor for over eight days, while never going to the liquor store.

Their campaign was on.

One afternoon, on one of the five days before the funeral, I was showering and I began to sing. My singing triggered my father's memory of his childhood experience of "moaning songs." In his youth, when there was a death, there would be a type of vigil held until the funeral. Neighbors and family members would come to visit, and join in the singing of these songs. Apparently, Daddy hated it!

So, when he heard me singing in his drunken stupor, he began to yell out, "I don't want any 'mourning singin' up in here!"

That was Pooh's signal to protect Daddy, correct me, and put me in my place.

She came knocking hard on the bathroom door, and in an authoritative voice announced, "Your Daddy don't want no singing in the house."

I was so heated that I almost didn't need to dry off, but I held my peace. In retrospect, I would come to realize that I was experiencing the good cop, bad cop routine. Given the ease with which these sisters flowed in their roles, these witches had done this before.

What eluded me was to what end? They had been my aunts for as far back as I could remember and had treated me with endearment. How was I to interpret their change of behavior? Who cut the ties that bind?

At the apex of my professional life, I was experiencing the nadir of my familial context. My rapid rise at Cargill was, in part, a function of my capacity to understand the conceptual framework of the crushing margin; to sell soy meal in various local geographies and coherently communicate marketing conditions.

My Blackness was also an accelerant. I was the lone Black merchant in the division and people approached me with inquisitiveness. But my current position at the Lake Office was a plumb of envy. Each soybean plant had at least one senior merchant position, responsible for soy meal sales in their territory. Soybean oil was a much smaller market, and therefore, was sold from a central desk, which was my current position. The soy oil market, in contrast to soy meal markets, was so small that very few trades were done directly between buyer and seller, and almost all trades were conducted through a broker.

Brokers held a unique role as purveyors of the market place. Buyers and sellers relied upon these brokers to ascertain market values and conditions. It was my role to sell the division's cash oil position at the highest base point possible, above the current futures market, as well as to have my finger on the pulse of the oil market. Is the market headed up or down? Is there liquidity of not? Is demand strong or weak? Who is the next anticipated export shipper and in what month? It was my responsibility to know the pulse.

It was also my responsibility on a daily basis to provide the division, and the broader company, with some indication of soy oil market conditions. This was accomplished through a daily wire that went out to all trading markets throughout the company, including abroad.

The daily wire might include a listing of the most current trades reported by brokers, but the Friday report was the most important. Here, one not only recanted significant trades during the week, but also provided insight into the tone, texture, and direction of the market. As 99% of traders were white males, and most were under the age of 50, I would entice my readers through the use of some sexual connotation.

This might include for instance, "The market is so hot, I find myself panting!"

Or, on another occasion in slower trading conditions I might write, "The market feels like an old spinster who remembers what it feels like to make a trade, but it's been a while!"

Well, needless to say, misogynistic terminology among white males in the late 1970s was like candy to a baby. If my Friday oil wire did not go out by 3 p.m., I would get a call from the traders in Amsterdam checking to see if they had missed it, because they wanted to read it before they left the office for the weekend.

However, with all of this popularity, I was without a mentor to help ensure my current and future success in the company. Palmby, now a manager of the Eastern Division of the plants, worked only three desks away from me. He was not my mentor, even though I had worked for him in Cedar Rapids. I think I had missed an opportunity for another mentor when I was invited to an after-work dinner party hosted by one of the vice presidents of the company on the second floor of the Lake Office. If I remember correctly, a family conflict prevented my attendance. I was thoroughly embarrassed and clueless when I realized its importance. I asked Donna, the central receptionist, regarding the protocol at this point. She explained that a note to the host apologizing for my absence would be appropriate. Who knew? I was glad I asked!

Besides being emotionally distraught due to my mother's death, I was equally distraught being away from my job without a mentor to call. I was in complete internal conflict.

When Lydia arrived, she was of little help. In that way that married people communicate with each other without vocalization, she let me know that there was nothing in my parent's house that she valued. She made it clear that from her perspective, my top priority should be to return to Minnesota, resume my position, and provide for our family.

I was also grieving the dismantling of both my mother and father's accomplishments. Momma and Daddy had worked so hard for so many years, and Daddy in his current state was in no position to hold things together.

Poor Daddy. He had lost his best friend and lover. Alcohol had always been his way to self-medicate, and given this loss, he needed as much medication as he could get.

Daddy carried the stupor with him as we visited the funeral home to pick out the casket and flowers, and to veto my more expensive taste, commenting, "Your Momma and I don't believe in putting a lot of money in the ground."

My communication with Daddy was minimal during that week, but I felt so strongly that I should do something. But what? I could not let his sisters, my aunts, just run over me. After all, I am the son, and the only child. I called my mother's brother, Uncle Henderson, for some advice. His advice was to "just stay cool."

He said, "After the funeral, pack your bags, take your wife, and go home to your son."

Interestingly enough, it was the same advice I received from Uncle Henry,

Pooh's husband, which he gave me at the end of the funeral, as he was next to Pooh when she pushed the church door on me.

Uncle Henry had said, "Stay cool and keep your head."

It made no sense at the time. I simply could not hear them. Not only could I barely walk, I could barely think. I did not recognize that in all of this milieu of silence and deception, I was the target. For, "If you can bind the strongman, you can take the house."

This silence prevented any agreed upon plan of action. These aunts were not interested in negotiating with me regarding how to resolve the family dilemma; they were not interested in compromise. They wanted it all. They knew the pressure I was under. They knew the attitude of my wife. They knew I had to return to my job. So, their plan was to heighten the tension between Daddy and me, and thereby advance their standing.

By the following Monday morning, I had determined my plan of action and started the implementation. I called the police. Upon their arrival, I told them that my mother had died and that my father was mentally incompetent and needed to be placed in a facility. They said they could take him in, but we would need the approval of a judge for placement.

Blanche, Pooh, and I stood in the living room, watching the police pull Daddy from the floor and handcuff him. The adrenaline rushing through my veins was so intense, I thought I might pass out. My testicles felt like they had fallen into my shoes. I'm not sure if it was visible or not, but I was shaking from the inside out. I knew, in that moment, that I had made a life-altering decision with no idea of the outcomes it would produce. Needless to say, there was silence.

We all got in the car and followed the police to the courthouse, continuing in silence. When our case was called, I explained to the Judge the circumstance and my dilemma. My speech was broken, my delivery was erratic, and I'm sure I appeared frustrated.

Blanche asked to speak and gave the most eloquent, silver-tongued summary of the circumstance that I had ever heard her deliver in life. She acknowledged that my father had a drinking problem, that he lost his companion of over 30 years, and was in a state of mourning. She concluded by saying that though she lived in Chicago, she was in a position to stay in Norfolk and assist her brother until a proper supportive arrangement was found.

Pooh nodded her head and intimated that she too would stay and help her brother. I knew I had lost.

The Judge questioned Daddy, asking his occupation and home address. Then he asked if Daddy had paid his taxes on the house. Daddy responded in the positive. The Judge concluded that Daddy was not mentally ill in need of placement, but obviously had a drinking problem, and given the resource of his two sisters, the Judge, in one fell swoop dismissed the case and my position in the family.

We returned to the homestead in silence. Once inside, Daddy said he thought it best if I packed my bags and went back to Minnesota. I had achieved the status of persona non grata. I went home.

Aunt Blanche was true to her word. She stayed at the homestead for about three months. Aunt Pooh, not so much. Her enthusiasm eroded with every soiled pair of pants they had to clean up. In less than a month, Pooh was back in New York. Blanche and Daddy agreed that he would move to an assisted living facility only blocks away, in the same community. Our family doctor had converted his former home to assisted living, so Daddy was in walking distance to the homestead. With that agreement in place, Blanche proceeded to dismantle the house. She sold everything she could.

Momma, being a Church Lady, was a serious dresser. She had suits and hats for days, not to mention formal gowns and shoes. Every room in the house was fully furnished. When Blanche held the estate sale, all of Momma's friends and neighbors stopped in, including Betty, Momma's boss from the elementary school. Betty would later comment to me on Blanche's savvy approach in selling Daddy's belongings. Blanche sold everything she could. She could not get the price she desired for the Mediterranean dining room set and Momma and Daddy's bedroom set, so she had those pieces shipped to her home in Chicago.

It goes without saying that Blanche helped Daddy write a will. Momma and Daddy had not seen any purpose in wills because our family was small. By Virginia law, what Momma had would automatically fall to Daddy, and Daddy's possessions would fall to me. There was a cousin on the Lewis side of the family who also lived in Norfolk. Blanche made him Executor of the Estate. With that in order, Blanche returned to Chicago.

A year would pass before I returned to Norfolk. I went to see Daddy to check up on how he was doing. He was living at the doctor's assisted living facility and he was obviously struggling health-wise. He had the shakes and I watched as a nurse gave him a small glass of wine. He could barely get the glass to his lips; he was shaking so badly. We had very little to say to each other. It felt very much like I was no longer his son, but simply a stranger to him.

Three more years would pass before I went back to Norfolk again. This time, Daddy was no longer in the residential facility. I went there first, looking for him. I called Blanche and asked where he was staying. She did not have the exact address, but she called her cousin and he gave me the address, only a few blocks down the street from Mt. Olive Baptist Church. I took off to find him.

When I found the house, I thought it strange that no one answered the doorbell. I tried the door, and it was open. The floor of the house was completely empty. The house was in rough shape as the paint was peeling from the walls. It was a spacious single-family dwelling with a large living room that flowed into the dining room and to the left the kitchen.

I called out, "Hello," but there was no response.

I decided to go upstairs. At the top of the stairs and to the right was an open door to one of the bedrooms. When I crossed the threshold, I got this sense of vertigo, a sense of movement of whirling as if the room was moving. It was not, of course. Then I realized what it was — roaches. Roaches everywhere. Roaches crawling the walls, window, and floor. There was Daddy, lying flat on a mat, covered to his neck with a smutty, filthy blanket and a pillow under his head, covered with roaches. Roaches crawling across his face.

He had suffered a stroke. When he saw my face, he began to talk, but the stroke had affected his speech and his words sounded as if he was speaking under water, with a kind of gurgling sound. My heart was broken.

I immediately began to apologize, "Daddy, I'm so sorry that they are doing this to you, but there is nothing that I can do."

I ran from the house back to my rented car, and cried.

I called Blanche and said to her, "I went to see Daddy. He was in an empty house with roaches crawling all over him. He doesn't deserve that!"

She said she would call her cousin.

■ ■ ■

Several more years would pass, with minimal contact with Blanche, and no contact with Daddy. One Thursday morning, I got a call from Betty, Momma's former boss. I knew what had happened when I heard her voice.

She said, "Arthur, I'm calling because your Daddy died and the funeral is tomorrow. And I didn't know if they contacted you."

I inquired about her health and thanked her for her call. What to do next?

I took an early morning direct flight from Minneapolis to Norfolk. I went straight to the Office of Records and asked how I might stop a funeral.

The woman behind the desk said, "The only way to do that is if you are the next of kin."

I replied that I was. She had me take an oath swearing that I was telling the truth. With that, she entered an injunction to stop the funeral, and had it delivered by the police.

I took my time getting to the funeral home because I wanted to enter after the injunction had been delivered. When the police officers came out the front door, I got out of the car and headed inside. As I opened the door, coming down the hallway in front of me was Blanche. I grabbed her and hugged her and asked if she was okay. She was trembling, but told me she was alright. I apologized for my actions, but said they had run over me long enough and that I am the next of kin.

What the injunction interrupted was the family gathering to ride to the church for the funeral. Daddy's body was already there. As I walked into the parlor area, his two sisters, Pooh and Lucy, were seated. All the people gathered had been told that the funeral had been halted and would not be held until the following Monday.

Some women were crying over the disruption, and I heard one of them say, "There he is. He is the son!"

The woman at the Office of Records was only partially correct. I was able to stop the funeral because I was the next of kin, and no will had been filed. Aunt Blanche was extremely skillful. She really did not intend on sharing portions of the estate evenly with her sisters. I speculated that once Daddy had been buried, she would argue that most of the money had been consumed in the cost of his care, so the estate was only a fraction of what it was originally. Without filing the will, Blanche could, in effect, give the sisters a few thousand dollars each, while retaining the balance. But by my asserting my legal position, she had to file the will in order to maintain control over the estate.

After the shattering of family and friends at the funeral home, I headed toward the church. That's when things got even more interesting. I went straight to the pastor's office. It immediately became clear that there was a new pastor, a young man also from North Carolina. From his speech pattern, he appeared to be moderately educated at best.

I introduced myself as the son of Leon Tredwell, the body lying in repose in the sanctuary. I told him portions of the family situation, and that I regrettably had to stop the funeral. He lost it! Fortunately for me, there were also two deacons present in his office, as I explained my position. The pastor became so upset, he lunged over his desk to hit me, but the deacons restrained him. We had never met each other and I could not immediately understand the source of his anger.

After a while, the reason occurred to me. He was a new pastor after all, and the church had engaged in significant preparation for the wake, the funeral, and a meal of repass for the family to be served after they returned from the gravesite. This now was all canceled. He thought he would be blamed for this confusion, and I was the cause! After that narrow escape, I came out into the sanctuary and saw a number of Daddy's relatives from his town of origin, Creswell.

I went over to greet them and to apologize for the disruption. They weren't having it. These relatives had made the hour-long drive, and they did not intend to come back on Monday. I simply expressed to them my regrets, and noted that I am the son and it was well within my rights to make that change.

I got the sense from them that they never considered me to be Leon's son.

For these people, there was a significant difference between adoption and blood, particularly as it related to money.

■ ■ ■

Generational robbery and legacy interruption within the Black family is a horrible occurrence. For the adoptee, the intentional disruption is often more painful than the economic loss, because the act negates historical operative understandings of relationality, even as It disrupts one's core sense of identity.

Blanche was my favorite aunt for 26 years. She and Boe had provided a place of solace when my adoption was disrupted. How could she do what she did? Did she not love me? Did she not love her brother, my father, whom she also betrayed? Where was the love? Or, was this the pinnacle of a 24-year-long charade? How do I wear this new badge of Black-Queer-male-disinherited-adoptee?

I am a Believer and I have been faithful to my calling. But where is God when you need Him/Her? How was He/She working this half-a-million-dollar embezzlement out to my good? What kind of stepping stone or building block of the lived experience was this?

What gain was this psychological/spiritual trauma intended to provide?

This memoir that I have shared harkens back to my first 30 years of life. While more than 30 years have passed since these recorded lived experiences have happened, there have been many gains and additional losses along the journey. I remain a Believer and testify that the God of the biblical text is faithful. To date, I have not been able to manifest the "mega-church" of my dreams and preferred future. Nor, have I been able to sustain an intimate committed relationship with a male or a female. Yet, I still declare that God is faithful.

In 1969, Dr. James Cone utilized the historically famous Exodus narrative, *The Deliverance of Israel from Egyptian Bondage*, as the biblical basis for his theological reflections on Black Theology and Black Power. In his book by the same title, Cone distinctly defines the context of the African American experience and the resulting Theology of the Black Church. His work liberated a whole new way of thinking and writing Theologically.

Twenty-four years later, in 1993, Dr. Delores Williams wrote *Sisters in the Wilderness*. Dr. Williams breathes life and racial humanity into the elevated character of Hagar, the hand-maiden of Abraham, and Sarah, the surrogate mother of Ishmael, the firstborn of the promise. Williams engages Hagar metaphorically to tell the lived experience of many African American women. Too frequently, these are stories of survival and defiance. In expositing this narrative, Williams advances a particular Theology - Womanist Theology. A Theology that emerges from the interconnectedness of oppression and its on-going impact on the intersectionality of race, class, gender, and sex.

Now, 31 years after *Sisters in the Wilderness*, I submit for your consideration a subjugated biblical story divided between the 38th and 39th chapters of the book of Jeremiah. A brief, yet powerful, narrative recorded by Baruch Ben Neriah, scribe to the prophet Jeremiah. In this story we see Yahweh call, persuade, plan, plot, implement and ultimately bless a Black Queer male. This is the bible story and its metaphorical understanding which is not taught in Sunday school or Bible study.

II.

The
Word of the
Lord Came to me
Saying...

7

I didn't do the writing...but He signed my name.
—Traditional

Is there no balm in Gilead; Is there no physician there? Why then is not the health of the daughter of my people recovered? (Jeramiah 8:22)

Practical Black Queer Theology, our sense of God and the spirituality that Black men and women practice daily, "on the ground while you are still around," may be understood as our incessant analyzing and synthesizing of: 1) our lived experience, 2) the text we deem sacred, and 3) the hermeneutics or lens by which we interpret these holy texts. This unceasing process essential to our survival operates at the personal and the communal levels. As I further this discussion, I will refer to Black biblical truth-seeking individuals as Believers and our communal religious expressions as the worship experience of Black Churches.

Believers and Black Churches live out their faith in the geographical and sociopolitical context of the United States of America. A nation mythicized as among the greatest of all civilizations; a colonized nation whose foundational wealth was achieved, and is sustained, by slavery - unpaid, underpaid, and the migrant labor of Black, Brown, Red, poor, and middle-class white peoples.

In recent years, we as a society have been forced to acknowledge that our dominating narrative of "life, liberty, and justice for all" has fallen deeper and deeper into decrepitude as the fallacy of this mantra is repeatedly proven. A nation so bedazzled by whiteness and the bottomless privileges of the conservative white male can barely envision holding a four-timed, criminally-indicted president, with a total of 88 charges, accountable for his blatant and overt lawlessness. This occurs as Black men and women are falsely arrested and shot to death in their cars and apartment doorways, without the recitation of their Miranda rights. A nation whose elites, "the one-percent," openly negate the voting process by their wealth, and in so doing, catapult the 99% into a future of racial injustice, open violence, and relentless discrimination impacting all "others" who are not born as wealthy white males.

Because the forces and voices of the colonized mind are so ever-present in our society, Blackness and its meaning are constantly under threat. There are constant forces negating our existence. These negating forces strip away our individuality and seek to reduce us to a single constituency. In alignment with the colonized mind, forces that readily seek to articulate what we are not. We are not this, and we are not that. Our history is declared to be without value in the state of Florida.

Sociologically, our present is unstable given our two-tiered justice system and, therefore, the prognosis of our future is questionable. Informed Black Believers and progressive Black Churches recognize these tenets as historical deceptions, rooted in white supremacy and the fruit of the spirit of dominance.

With time, it becomes clear that the nature of our sociopolitical existence has a cyclical dimension. Today, 60 years removed from Bayard Rustin's salvation of the Montgomery Boycott, his conception of the Southern Christian Conference, and his facilitation of the March on Washington, we appear to have unintentionally returned to another season of Truth. We capitalize the word to reflect a transcendent fundamental or spiritual reality. In this season of Truth, "purported Truths" such as "One nation under God," implode and disintegrate by the intrinsic weight of their artificiality. Truth is, one can only build on authenticity!

Consider the following historical Black Church Theological corrective. On January 23, 2024, the Reverend Dr. Gina Marcia Stewart became the first Black woman to preach in the Joint Board Session of the National Baptist Convention. The convention is a 129-year-old institution. Dr. Stewart's preaching is hailed as a progressive milestone, even as her celebration ignores the subjugation, degradation, and destruction of the ministerial callings of millions of Black women over the last 13 decades. While fully acknowledging the symbolic nature of her preaching event, I mourn the millions of Black women preachers, those living and the dead on whose graves she stands.

I mourn the loss of their congregational affirmation. I mourn their loss of institutional recognition. I mourn the ambivalence of their social location, caught between the internal demands of a profound undeniable spiritual calling that compelled them to stare down cultural, socio-political negation and institutional dismissal. I mourn their vast creativity, their genius, and their transformative understandings that never saw the light of day because they were born, swathed in fertile black-skinned flesh, possessing breasts and vaginas.

> *Oh, that my head were waters, and mine eyes a fountain of tears, that I might weep day and night for the slain of the daughter of my people!* (Jeremiah 9:1)

A key to understanding this prolonged female subjugation is to remember that the formation of the Black Church provided the opportunity to nurture and advance the leadership development of the straight Black male. While patriarchy supplies the justification and purported truths supporting the diminishing of Black female leadership, the Black Church's greatest anathema is not the Black female. It is the Black Queer male as preacher/pastor. Trust me, homophobia among Black preachers "of a certain age" is a much greater negating force than patriarchy, though patriarchy also has its role. Together, they constitute a dual negation whose energies are deeply rooted in fear.

What cannot be ignored in this discussion is the acidic level of virulence, bitter hostility, and rancor subjected to the personage of Queer Black males seeking the pastorate in Black Churches. This bitterness seems to be especially prevalent among minimally trained and undereducated Black clergy. This ideology is most rampant among insecure church founders, generally identifiable as operating from a stance of "My way or the highway!"

I have known pastors who have "exiled" their gay biological sons from their families of origin. I, myself, have been called a "faggot" in the pulpit. I have been told I would never amount to anything because I was cursed with a curse! This incident occurred during Sunday morning worship, as the choir and congregation sang, "O, How I Love Jesus."

Conversely, another pastor advised me to fight against my homosexual inclinations exclaiming, "You have to fight against it...you have to fight...you have to fight...," as he forcefully slammed his fist on the desk, and stated in conclusion, "You need to get away from me. You are too gifted and I don't want to be responsible for your destruction. And I can't help myself."

I left. It would later come to light that he had sexually molested his daughter, his firstborn child.

What gives these Black pastors the license and permission to be fully confident in their righteous indignation, and their willful destruction of another human being?

Among the many contributing factors, we must include positional insecurity, sexual insecurity, and internalized Black self-hatred. All of these come to mind. However, from a biblical perspective, I suggest their springboard is their literal interpretation of the word, abomination, taken from the Levitical text. An abomination is something detestable, morally repugnant, a disgrace, an obscenity, something cursed, evil, an anathema, a monstrosity, something or someone to be hated, something offensive in the eyes of God. Is there any greater surety of righteousness than to hate what one knows God hates?

But what if these abusive dehumanizing Black pastors are wrong, like those Theologians who espoused the theory that Black people lived under the curse of Ham? Or, their erroneous interpretation of Scripture affirming their Theologically based subjugation of women? What if there is a biblical narrative that completely contradicts their pervasive narrative of degradation? What if there is a biblical narrative where God, Yahweh, in partnership with a Black Queer trans male persuades, plots, plans, implements, and blesses a strategic rescue of one of Yahweh's servants? A servant that happens to be the manifested Word of God. A narrative that straight white male and female commentators noticed, but could not relate, so they passed over its exposition.

What if, in all of these years, Believers have been misinformed, hoodwinked, bamboozled, and led astray? What are the implications of such Truth, not only for Boomers, but for Generation X, Millennials, Generation Z, and Alphas?

The Book of Jeremiah contributes significantly to our liberation Theological stance as it opens, by offering us a surrogate creation narrative in Jeremiah Chapter One:

¹ The words of Jeremiah the son of Hilkiah, of the priests that
were in Anathoth in the land of Benjamin
² To whom the word of the Lord came in the days of Josiah the son
of Amon king of Judah, in the thirteenth year of his reign.
³ It came also in the days of Jehoiakim the son of Josiah king of
Judah, unto the end of the eleventh year of Zedekiah the son of
Josiah king of Judah, unto the carrying away of Jerusalem captive
in the fifth month.
⁴ Then the word of the LORD *came unto me saying,*
⁵ Before I formed thee in the belly I knew thee; and before thou
camest forth out of the womb I sanctified thee, and I ordained
thee a prophet unto the nations.

In his first prophetic utterance, Jeremiah has his scribe, Baruch ben Neri-ah, record his biological identity as the son of the priest, Hilkiah. Their family lives in Anathoth, a city three miles north of Jerusalem. Jeremiah prophesied for 40 years and he identified the kings of Judah under which he served. He distinguishes his voice from that of Yahweh, introducing his prophetic formu-la, articulating for us a surrogate creation narrative.

⁴ Then the word of the LORD *came unto me saying,*
⁵ Before I formed thee in the belly I knew thee; and before thou
camest forth out of the womb I sanctified thee, and I ordained
thee a prophet unto the nations.

This verse is among the most profound verses in all the biblical text. It sug-gests that humankind is created and conceived in a recognizable, knowable form prior to its encasement in a body. This essence of humankind existed before eyes, mouth, teeth, limbs, skin, or internal organs were ordered and arranged. Further, not only did we exist in this de-materialized state, but we were individually distinguishable and identifiable, and most profoundly, we were in a relationship and known by God.

One radical dimension of this passage purports a de-emphasis on the centrality of the physical body to the experience of life. Further, it infers an individual and unique relationship with the Divine, prior to our transformation of physical birth. Jeremiah suggests that prior to any physical manifestation, we existed as a spiritual essence. A status I summarize as "nameless but known."

The power of this passage is that it moves us Theologically from a bodily focus and the discussions of molded clay and side ribs, snakes and fruit, human hierarchy, patriarchy, and the centrality of the colonized mind, where all are defined by bodily elements of melanin or its absence, breasts, vaginas, and penises. It is this bodily emphasis, coupled with Black self-hatred, that is also the root of much of the Black Church's high sin consciousness. Unfortunately, for many Black people, biblical negation correlates with societal negation, reinforcing internalized Black self-hatred.

Jeremiah proceeds to announce that once conceived in our de-materialized, nameless state, the Creator then sanctifies us unto God's self. In Pentecostalism, we are taught that sanctification is a process of drawing nearer and closer to a state of holiness. Further, the gift of the baptism in the Holy Ghost is the seal of God upon a sanctified life. Yet, Jeremiah suggests that we are sanctified before the transformation of birth. Not only are we sanctified before the birth experience, but we are also called to a particular purpose. I submit that there is a strong correlation between the nature of our energies and the purpose to which we are called.

The unaddressed question of this biblical text is if we were nameless and known, how did God know us, and how did God distinguish between us?

I submit and believe the text moves us toward a realization that our truest essence is not our body. Rather, our truest essence is our energy - our life force. I submit that God knows us by our energy. There are several lived experiences, as well as scientific implications, supportive of such an understanding.

A close friend of mine recently lost his father. We will call him David. David is 50 years old and his father was in his 80s. His father died overnight in the family home. The next morning when David tried to rouse his father, he said that he knew his father had transitioned before he even touched him.

"His energy was gone," David said, with an intuitive knowing.

The next day, his brother, who lives some distance from the house, came over.

His immediate observation to David upon entering the family home was, "The energy in this house is completely different."

Perhaps you have experienced this as well. I have observed people from a distance; people with good reputations, upstanding and recommended to be known. Yet, when the opportunity for close proximity occurred, I observed something about their energy that was intuitively incongruent with my own.

Science approaches this issue from a conservation of energy theory. This theory formulates that energy can neither be created nor destroyed by humankind, but can be transformed. If this is correct, then our energy has only one source - our Creator. That it cannot be destroyed reinforces theologies of eternal life, while its transformative capacities imply possibilities for work, movement, change, redirection, and reification.

If Jeremiah is Truth, then Yahweh is more concerned with how we use our innate energy and how we discover and achieve our purpose. Godly concerned, as to how in our humanity we come to value our uniquely designed energy that He/She has placed in us...before we were embryos. That Yahweh, who stands at the starting post and the finishing line, may be more concerned about our journey to the self, and the achieving of our purpose, than He/She is regarding our physicality, which Jeremiah views as temporal. For, we existed prior to our encasement.

Queer Folx, you weren't born this way...you were created this way!

The white colonial mindset places all of our essence in the body. From their perspective, to enslave the bodies of others is to achieve socio-political dominance. This construct was disproven years ago. This dominating narrative of the early 20th century faced its most public socio-political unraveling with Hitler in the 1936 Olympics.

African Americans were under the foot of Jim Crow when Jesse Owens defeated all of the white track stars that year. Run Jesse, run! Even before Jesse, and down through the years, despite the brutality of slavery, the energies of Black folks have continuously invented and created superlative contributions, in diverse disciplines, to the benefit of all humankind; demonstrations of energy over flesh. This leads us to consider the mystery of the Black Church worship experience.

On April 17, 1960, Dr. Martin Luther King, Jr. said in a "Meet the Press" Interview, "...11:00 on Sunday morning is one of the most segregated hours, if not the most segregated hour, in Christian America."

This has been repeated innumerable times over the decades.

Whenever I hear this quote, I always find myself saying under my breath, "But there's a reason for that..."

A reason that speaks profoundly to the different racial identities and spiritual needs of both Blacks and whites. Having pastored predominantly white congregations in more than one instance, my generalized experience suggests that each community gathers for distinctly different reasons, expectations, and outcomes.

For my white Christian brothers and sisters, church attendance is an opportunity for communal engagement. Satisfying the need to belong reinforces the sense of the familial, emphasizing ritual and fellowship. For some, Sunday morning worship at 11 a.m. is the prelude to brunch where the fellowship is extended and there is an opportunity for libations. Broadly speaking, worship in the white congregations I have observed appears to be an activity that is provided, not necessarily an activity in which one engages. It has never been clear to me that there has been any anticipation of the 'move of the spirit' or anticipation of any particular spiritually related outcomes.

The emotionality of Black Church worship has long been rejected by the dominating culture and white protestant stoicism. Such rejection is simply a pile-on as one more negation of Blackness and/or our Africanisms. But for the Believer, there is a direct connection between Sunday morning worship and their Monday through Saturday night experience.

Traditional Black Church worship, back in the day, and to a limited extent presently, began with "Devotional Service," generally conducted between 15 and 30 minutes before structural worship, providing an opportunity for individual participation. Congregants would stand and, when recognized, might lead the congregation into singing their favorite song, and then give their testimony. Their testimony might be a statement of thanksgiving or a summary of their current challenges. In conclusion, the individual might ask the church for prayer. Theologically, personal testimony may be understood as a current news flash as to what God is doing and how God is moving in their community, affirming and reinforcing a communal belief that God is presently active in the community's lived experience.

Black women constitute more than 80% of the Black Church population, so they almost always comprise a majority of worship participants on any given Sunday at almost any given Black Church. As the nation is learning, given the candidacy of Kamala Harris, Black women possess a certain undeniable energy and power. Teresa N. Washington, an African American academic, author, activist, and public speaker is known for her research on Aje, a Yoruba term that defines a spiritual power inherent in African women and others who have that power. African women possessing Aje, while often erroneously called witches, are in fact astrally-inclined human beings who enforce earthly and cosmic laws.

A long-standing friend and resident of Chicago, Dr. Gwen, tells this story of the power of her mother's prayers. Dr. Gwen's mother, Rosetta, gave birth to 14 children, unfortunately losing two - one to an illness at three years of age, and the last baby was stillborn. At the time, the family lived in Cabrini Green. For those who may not know Chicago, Cabrini Green was a concentration of low-income housing comprised of over 580 units of affordable housing located on the Near North Side of Chicago.

One day, Rosetta and a few of her children arrived home only to discover that the screen door to their unit was locked. Rosetta had the key to the front door, but no key had ever been needed for the screen door. She and the children were exhausted. They had been out all day running errands, and everybody was tired and hungry, and now another challenge presented itself. Rosetta, a powerful woman of prayer and faith, possessing Aje, quieted the children and brought them into a spirit of prayer. With every head bowed as they stood around the door, she began to pray a prayer similar to this:

"Lord, I am right now faced with an impossible situation. There is no money for a locksmith to call to resolve this issue. I have no other resource to call on but you. We have been out all day and I need to be able to get in the house to cook and feed these babies. I know that there is nothing too hard for you to do. I am asking you, in the name of Jesus... to open this screen door."

"We heard the lock 'click!'" said Dr. Gwen. "Momma opened the screen door, unlocked the front door, and we went in the house,"

The outcome Rosetta's prayer achieved is not witchcraft, but rather a function of a spiritual capacity to exercise the very definition of energy - to cause movement or change!

My conceptualized articulation of Rosetta's prayer parallels the prayers of most Believers, individual and communal, whether in private or corporately gathered for worship. Daily, we are faced with situations that are almost impossible to comprehend. We encounter people who have internalized all of the negativities associated with our melanin, rooted in the colonized mindset. In the moment of the encounter, there are no resources for us to call upon to counter their discriminatory actions. Or, we encounter people whose privilege has sheltered them from interfacing with Blacks, and we are forced to be polite in situations of ignorance and stupidity. Some approach us from a mythological sense of who we are. One example is some dentists who think there is no need to apply an oral anesthetic, because they believe Blacks can endure more pain than other individuals.

And, if it were not enough to have to endure these encounters with traditional whiteness, infused with issues of supremacy, we also must find ways to strive with the internalized self-hatred of Blacks. Black adults whom the educational and religious system failed; Blacks who have been undereducated, miseducated, and misled into illogical frameworks of understanding, both secular and sacred. And Blacks without a knowledge of self or self-love. Who, then in turn, have miseducated their own children. Thus, producing children with an uncertainty about their survival, and therefore, rendering fundamental education as not having value.

What resources do we have to counter this madness?

Social workers talk endlessly, but articulate very few solutions. Politicians make endless promises to no avail. Systemically, we are deceived by a cyclical tripartite governmental system that only works to delay and deter any socioeconomic progress of the middle and lower class. Daily, we find ourselves up against unrelenting forces whose pursuit is to deny the marginalized the basic tenants of citizenship. Forces that restrain our sense of self, power, and giftedness.

So, When Black people gather for worship, most Believers come "standing in the need" of a God encounter; needing a worship experience not to observe, but to engage. We come willing to employ our agency, offering our energies to achieve our desired spiritual outcome. To hear the unlocking of that which has been repressed, oppressed, and subjugated, bringing clarity to our hearts and clouded minds - click! To achieve this spiritual outcome, we raise Juba - the celebration of our life force and its connection to the Divine.

We gather to multiply vibrations. Vibrations we radiate into the atmosphere through our skilled instrumentation of guitars, pianos, pipe and Hammond organs, flutes and saxophones, trumpets and trombones, and the multiplicity of rhythms and polyrhythms produced by drums: snare, cymbals, babs, bongos, cajón and the djembe. All further accentuated by the clapping of hands, dancing of feet, and the vibrato of our voices. Voices which range in timbre and texture, tone and pitch, inclusive of that which is bright, dark, full, powerful, breathy, soft, velvety, mellow to nasal to raspy.

All further accentuated by shrills, screams hollers, moans, groans, the clapping of hands, the shuffle of dancing feet. We raise these vibrations as community, transferring energy to each other until there is an atmospheric shift, until there is spiritual saturation with the power to change, move, and heal in the present. Communally, we realign and reinvigorate our individual energies toward our uniquely called purposes.

Somewhere before the last dancer leaves the floor or the last shout is exalted, when the Spiritual Priests intuit that Juba has been achieved, they will signal and begin to reduce the level of vibrational intensity. Inducing a mellowing of the spiritual dynamic through a soothing melodic intervention. In Pentecostalism, there might be a turn to the spiritual anthem of Bishop Charles Harrison Mason – "Yes, Lord! My soul says yes!"

Among the Baptists, a singing pastor might lift a common meter such as, "Father, I stretch my hand to Thee...no other help I know."

And gingerly and sweetly, the intense transitions into tranquil. And even in the tranquil, healing, deliverance, and transformation is still occurring. But, in this phase of Juba, our hearts and minds are being opened, elevated, and prepared to hear and receive a word from God. A God-given word. A word of Truth. A word of empowerment and encouragement. A biblically-based word that speaks to our context of the impossible. A word that nurtures our survival. A word declaring..."Thus sayeth the Lord..."

But, before the Word, the choir sings...

8

Father in Heaven...let Your will be done.
—Traditional

Our text this morning comes from the book of Jeremiah, a revered prophetic book of the Hebrew Scriptures. A book, that on the one hand is disruptive and disjointed in content, yet, if we press our way, we will find it to be profoundly revelatory and even medicinal. It possesses a healing quality. That is, of course, as with all medicines...if we can take it in.

Black folks, people of African extraction, ought to give the book some special consideration because if one does, one will discover that while the book is not necessarily Black-centered, it has what might be regarded as Black Tendencies.

I offer the "laments" as a preliminary example. The "laments" parallel our Spirituals. Jeremiah, agonizing in the midst of the pain and suffering resulting from the loss of the kingdom, asks the question:

> *Is there no balm in Gilead, is there no physician there? Where*
> *then is not the health of the daughter of my people recovered?*
> *(Jeremiah 8:22)*

The enslaved of African descent responded to Jeremiah's question saying, "There is...a balm in Gilead, to heal the sin-sick soul!"

In the year 1020 B.C.E, one thousand and twenty years before the birth of Christ, Yahweh God, following and answering the desires of the people of God, told Samuel, "Go, anoint Saul, king over Israel."

God allowed this, even though God never wanted Israel to have an earthly king. The children of Israel had a great desire to be like the other nations. God wanted to be their king, but Yahweh allowed them to experience their aspirations.

What Israel missed in their short-term thinking is what God knew from the beginning; all kings and kingdoms created by man will ultimately fall. If Israel had chosen Yahweh as their king, they would have lived in the only kingdom that is from everlasting to everlasting, without end. (Somebody say glory!)

Three hundred years from Saul's reign, in 722 B.C.E., the northern kingdom of Israel falls, destroyed by the Neo-Assyrian Empire. And now, 136 years later, 586 B.C.E., Babylon and its king, Nebuchadnezzar, conquer the southern kingdom of Israel and plunder its capital, Jerusalem.

One of the life-giving and life-sustaining attributes of the Word of God is its "dunamis," the Greek word for power. This power elevates and reinforces the biblical text as a superlative source of wisdom and knowledge. Though its stories and recorded histories precede us by hundreds, and even thousands of years, these narratives so keenly mirror and reflect our present human conditions, often, directly addressing the precise context in which we find ourselves. Such is the case in this narrative. For the book of Jeremiah centers around the fall of the kingdom of Israel and the socio-political, psychological, spiritual, and Theological implications arising from Israel's experience of annihilation. Can we talk?

First, the pending destruction was something one could have predicted, well ahead of time. In Israel's case, Nebuchadnezzar had come through Jerusalem in 596 B.C.E., ten years before the fulfillment of Jeremiah's prophecy of exile. It was because Jehoiakim, King of Israel, had refused to pay the tributes due to Babylon. Nebuchadnezzar and his army came through and stripped all the visible gold he could find in the city. He took the golden vessels of worship and did not stop there, but went as far as to strip the gold from the doorpost of Jerusalem's Temple, built by Solomon. Nebuchadnezzar deposed Jehoiakim and placed Zedekiah on the throne. Nebuchadnezzar took Jehoiakim hostage back with him to Babylon, along with 10,000 other Israelites. But there is the problem that links their situation to ours...

The people of Israel were facing the complete dissolution of their primary political institutions; Legislative, Judicial, and Executive. They were witnessing the loss of their dominating political narrative. Their situation of life in 586 B.C.E. parallels our current context, and this is why the Bible has power. For in the United States of America, in the year 2025, we too are faced with irrefutable evidence that our dominating political narrative, "One nation under God with liberty and justice for all," is a lie. A lie, perpetrated and reinforced by each branch of our current government. For decades, these same three governmental structures have long been fraught with suspicion. But, now having been presented with undeniable evidence, we can only conclude that these pillars of our governance have been compromised. Whether we want to admit it or not, we, as a nation, must contend with the erosion of our dominating political narratives, even though this knowledge throws us head-first into a context of anxiety and uncertainty, increasing our susceptibility to fear, both internal and external.

Yet, in 586 B.C.E., the more staggering loss for Israel was the desecration and destruction of the Temple. First, because Israel believed that Yahweh dwelt and lived as a manifested presence in the inner sanctum, the Holy of Holies. It was here that the Shekhinah, the light of God's presence, shone. With the Temple being destroyed, not one brick resting upon another, where is God?

Not only is God's presence thrown into question. If one believes, as they did in ancient times, that in warfare, the God of the victor is the stronger God, does this loss imply that Marduk, Babylon's god, is stronger than Yahweh? Israel is not only faced with the erosion of its dominating political narrative, the nation is also faced with the loss of its dominating theological narrative, the source of its identity, Israel: one who wrestles and prevails with God.

We now come to the pericope of this sermon, Jeremiah 38: 7-13 coupled with Jeremiah 39: 15-18. I want to quite literally employ some of God's methodology in our approach to this text. My proposed approach is God-like in that it will allow us to know the ending, from the beginning. Is that alright?

I, in fact, want to start the reading at the very last sentences of the last divine utterance found in Chapter 39, verse 18. In that 18th verse, we find the last sentence of that text which reads:

For I will deliver thee, and thou shall not fall by the sword,
But thy life shall be a prize/bonus/boon, an experience to be enjoyed:
Because thou hast put thy trust in me.

I want to hasten and emphasize that very last, causal clause, because it explains the reason for the action of the main clause. In other words, Yahweh is saying...

What I'm doing for you Ebed-Melech – the rescue and
salvation I am providing to you...
and the reason I'm blessing you,
and the reason you don't have to be afraid or fearful,
and the reason I'm bringing deliverance to the very

threshold of your doorway,

In the midst of the utter destruction of all of Jerusalem

is because...you have trusted in me!

Now, before you shout right there, understand this...

This idea of achieving "trust" is not an overnight accomplishment. And, for Yahweh to refer to it in this way, there is an ever so slight inference that there was a time when Ebed-Melech did not trust.

I don't know about you, but I sense and perceive the implications of a process at work. A process of persuasion toward the ultimate goals of trust and collaborative agency - leading to rescue, deliverance, survival, and salvation.

I see Ebed-Melech and Yahweh on the down-low. Who knew? Didn't nobody know?! Yahweh persuades, enlightens and empowers the trans man of his purpose and Divine Calling.

Anybody, under the sound of my voice, on the down-low with God right now? Not ready to go public with your relationship with the Divine. Not ready to say I'm saved and sanctified, baptized, and filled. Not ready to stand up and tell the world. But, God is talking to you, and you can hear God calling your name! Anybody?

Yes, I support the view that Ebed-Melech needed to be persuaded to engage in Yahweh's plan for Jeremiah's rescue, survival, and salvation. When the idea was first presented to Ebed-Melech, he was not immediately convinced of its viability. And why should he be?

For just as there are punitive Black preachers today, there were priests and Temple authorities following the Deuteronomy text that said, *No one whose testicles have been crushed or whose penis has been cut off may come into the assembly of the Lord.* (Deuteronomy 23:1)

Why would anyone be desirous to get involved in a dissolving religious system that fails to affirm their God-given humanity? However, it has been my experience that one's perspective changes in extraordinary ways when one comes to realize that the persistent and persuasive voice they are hearing is the voice of God. Has God ever spoken to you? Have you ever heard the Creator's voice? I don't want to tarry here, but just let me say...

> God speaks...and the sound of God's voice is so sweet, the birds
> hush their singing! And the melody, that God gives to me, within
> my heart, is ringing,
> And God walks with me and God talks with me, and God tells me
> I am God's own.
> And the joy, we share as we tarry there, none other has ever
> known.

Now, having glimpsed the ending and contemplative lens, let us go to the beginning of our pericope and engage the full narrative.

The King James Version reads:

> Now when Ebed-Melech the Ethiopian, one of the eunuchs which was in the king's house, heard that they had put Jeremiah in the dungeon; the king then sitting in the gate of Benjamin; Ebed-Melech went forth out of the king's house... (Jeremiah 38:7-8)

One of the reasons this narrative has been so easy to subjugate is that editors of this story have presented it in a very minimal manner. From the beginning, Ebed-Melech is portrayed as a very minor character, *"one of the eunuchs which was in the kings' house,"* which is a substantive misnomer, as the narrative ultimately proves. Ebed-Melech is not one of the eunuchs in the king's house. He is the master of the king's house. The constant repetition of stating his ethnicity (ultimately even by the voice of Yahweh) may also be a contributing factor leading a casual reader to interpret his socio-political status as "other." Yet, the historical relationship between Israel and Ethiopia is long-standing, with many indications that the two nations emerged from Egypt together in the Exodus.

The larger point is that Ebed-Melech did not just jump up and go to the king upon hearing of Jeremiah's plight. Rather, as we have discussed, he is employing his agency, having been persuaded of Yahweh.

In addition, Ebed-Melech is a highly developed leader when we are introduced to him. There are certain prerequisites to the level of advanced leadership he displays which should not be ignored. What is clear is that he holds the position of chief eunuch and master over the king's household, a position of power and influence. Whether immigrant or native, to arrive at such a trusted position in a colonized nation, by necessity, any subaltern would have engaged in the process of personal, emotional, and intellectual investigation. The transformative process through which any subaltern must pass to arrive at a concretized place of self-love and self-knowledge; both essential attributes and prerequisites to any position of informed advanced leadership - then and now.

No doubt, among Ebed-Melech's greatest psychological challenges was his journey to peace given the physical assault upon his body which prescribed his gender – the act of castration. The Bible is written from a hetero-normative position and eunuchs represent a third gender. Biblical commentators are quick to say that Jesus does not speak to issues of homosexuality. But, Jesus does speak of eunuchs in Matthew 19:12.

He says, *"For there are some eunuchs, which were so born from their mother's womb; and there are some eunuchs, which were made eunuchs of men; and there be eunuchs, which have made themselves eunuchs for the sake of the kingdom."*

Ebed-Melech was a eunuch made of men, even as Jesus was a eunuch for the sake of the kingdom.

In the sixth Century, C.E., an occasional pregnancy within a harem would be part of the natural order of things. Often, these children were birthed and reared as part of the aristocracy, particularly if the male children demonstrated high intellect or capabilities. They were, after all, royal babies; illegitimate sons (and daughters) of the king. This practice was observed as long as the male child presented no threat to the kingship.

A surefire way of permanently minimizing this threat was castration. Virility was an unwavering and essential characteristic of kingship, and therefore, castration was a complete disqualifier. This act carried a 20 percent rate of survival if both penis and testicles were removed, with the survival rate increasing slightly if only the testicles were removed. In either case, if the young lad survived, he could rise to any height attainable within the governance structure. Hell, he could even be chief eunuch over the king's household.

Ebed-Melech did have a royal quality permeating his character. He seemed to have known what was possible and he appeared to have possessed a strong intuitive sense of how to get things done. He was a political change agent. While fully aware of all protocols, he operated both within and outside of the parameters of his designated role. I find it amazing that his networking and informational systems were working and intact, alerting him to the status of occurrences throughout Jerusalem when everyone else, including the king, appeared to be in chaos. One must remember that Jerusalem had been under siege for eighteen months. All hell broke loose, and no one with certainty could distinguish between truth and fiction, information and disinformation.

Even the king had no idea what to expect as he was constantly asking the question, "Is there any word from the Lord?"

Yet, amidst this confused state, Ebed-Melech had a networking system that kept him accurately informed. Perhaps his networking system evolved due to the various messages that Ebed-Melech relayed to and from the king, requiring that he cross numerous and varied portals. The role of the messenger is a well-established function of a eunuch. This capacity implies that Ebed-Melech possessed and employed the attribute of liminality, which is also often noted among eunuchs throughout the ages. It is an ability to cross many thresholds, engage many voices, and always be welcomed back. So disruptive was this period, that the major Jeremiah scholars, Stulman, Carroll, Bright, and Brueggemann believe that the disjointed nature of the book of Jeremiah is a literary device utilized to reflect the disruptive context of the time.

When I read the opening sentence of this narrative, my personal interpretation is to say, "Nobody gave a damn about Jeremiah until Ebed-Melech heard about his plight! And he, persuaded by Yahweh, decided to intervene."

This is also a prophetic axiom alerting believers as to how dispassionately, without remorse or consciousness, governing political entities can discard and disregard the Word of God, particularly when there is a risk to their wealth, power and position, as was the case with the princes of Judah- Israel's one-percent.

It was this tension that led to Jeremiah being thrown into the cistern. Here, we also identify a second Blackish Tendency. Jeremiah was a powerfully dynamic preacher. Like Jeremiah, Black preachers have elevated the sermonic moment to an art form. Jeremiah would do whatever it took to convey his prophetic message as Truth. If he had to wear the yoke of an oxen, or a filthy girdle, or visit the potter's house and watch the artist form a new vessel, he would do whatever was necessary to impactfully proclaim the Word of God.

He preached so convincingly that the soldiers and guards, who functioned as the protective secret service for the one-percent, began to leave their post and voluntarily take the two-week journey into Babylon. Given their increasing risk of vulnerability, the one-percent demanded that Jeremiah be punished. They petitioned Zedekiah, the would-be-king, and he completely folded, saying he had no authority to prevent their actions. With no one wanting the blood of the prophet on their hands, throwing him in the cistern efficiently accomplished their desired end.

> *(Ebed-Melech) ... spake to the king saying, My lord the king, these men have done evil in all that they have done to Jeremiah the prophet, whom they have cast into the dungeon; and he is like to die for hunger in the place where he is: for there is no more bread in the city. (Jeremiah 38:8-9)*

Having accepted his call to rescue Jeremiah, Ebed-Melech began to strategize. To successfully scale a political wall in opposition to the princes of Judah, the master of the king's house needed a plan that liberated Jeremiah, even as it simultaneously protected his own life (I wish I had a politician in the house! They would tell you that often the issue is not the right or the wrong – it's the timing). And for Ebed-Melech, this was not the time for a solitary political move. An ally was needed, a powerful ally that was not in the palace. To successfully resolve this call for rescue on Jeremiah's behalf, and still remain safe, the servant of the king discerned that the solution to this problem rested on the authority of the king. Without having asked a living breathing being, he exercised his liminality and proceeded to the king, who sat at the Benjamin Gate holding court. Without introduction or being summoned, Ebed-Melech began to enunciate a social justice argument on Jeremiah's behalf. But among commentators, there was a great dispute as to precisely what he said to the king.

The Septuagint text states that without summons, or introduction, or even polite greeting to the king, Ebed-Melech walked up to the king as he was holding court at the Benjamin Gate and said, "You have done evil in what you have done to kill this man with hunger."

The Masoretic text includes the polite greeting, "My Lord, the King," but goes on to accuse the princes as if the king had no role in this decision, "These men have done evil in all that they did to Jeremiah the prophet by casting him into the cistern."

For me, the larger question is, does Ebed-Melech have a sufficient relationship with the king to have said, "You have done evil," directly and to the point, or should he have been polite to the king and accused others of an action in which the king had also participated?

When Nathan confronted David, Israel's first true king, regarding his adultery with Bathsheba and the murder of her husband, Uriah, he presented the king with a story of injustice that kindled David's anger and judgment. David became so angry at the injustice portrayed in the story that, without knowing the guilty party, he passed a death sentence against the man.

It is at this point, Nathan reveals to David...*thou art the man*, in II Samuel 12:1-7.

Ebed-Melech's words to the king are important, because they convey and clarify his role as a full character in this narrative, even as they infer a certain depth of relationship with the king. Openly saying to the king, "What you have done is evil," seems to point to a very deep and personal relationship with the king. Such a relationship was entirely possible, for this "servant of the king" and his master had an intimate relationship.

Ebed-Melech protected the women with whom the king slept with. He knew with whom the king slept last, when and where it took place. Dare I say, he knew the quality of the encounter? Perhaps, he had personally prepared both the woman and the bed in which they slept. He may also have had in mind the woman who was slated for the next encounter.

> *Then the king commanded Ebed-Melech the Ethiopian, saying, take from hence thirty men with thee, and take up Jeremiah the prophet out of the dungeon, before he die. So Ebed-Melech took the men with him, and went into the house of the king under the trea-sury, and took thence old cast clouts and old rotten rags, and let them down by cords into the dungeon to Jeremiah. And Ebed-Mel-ech the Ethiopian said unto Jeremiah, Put now these old cast clouts and rotten rags under thine armholes under the cords. And Jere-miah did so. So, they drew up Jeremiah with cords, and took him up out of the dungeon: and Jeremiah remained in the court of the prison. (Jeremiah 38:11-13)*

In *Eunuchs and the Royal Harem in Achaemenid Persia (559-331 B.C.E)*, Lloyd Llewellyn-Jones discusses the customs of Hebrew royal court and informs us that only representatives of the leading Persian families, the king's wife and the king's mother, were privileged to appear before the king without sum-mons. All others were required to make a formal request for an audience. Yet, without summons, Ebed-Melech made a social justice argument, suggesting to the king that the actions and behavior of the princes of Judah had been evil as it related to Jeremiah, emphasizing not only the imprisonment of Jeremiah in the cistern, but also *all that they have done*. (Jeremiah 38:9)

Chapter 37 records a prior incident where Jeremiah is prevented from leaving the city when he was thought to be surrendering to the Babylonians. Subsequently, he was turned over to the princes of Judah, who beat him and placed him in prison in Jeremiah 37:15. No doubt, Ebed-Melech also had this incident in mind in his summary of *all that they have done*.

Without question, Ebed-Melech understood the king at a profound level. So familiar was he with the mind of the king that he innately understood the appropriateness of a direct-indirect strategy of persuasion. Ebed-Melech was direct in updating the king concerning the plight of the prophet, having directly asserted the perilous nature of the prophet's circumstance while having indirectly requested the king's assistance. Even though he pointed out the "evil" done by the princes, he never asked that they be punished or that Jeremiah be removed from the cistern. He left the argument open-ended, and placed all of the authority for solving the problem in Zedekiah's hands. Perhaps, what we are witnessing is a lesson in speaking truth to power.

Ebed-Melech, mission accomplished, proudly advanced the 30 soldiers he had been provided to assist and protect him as he marched through the city of Jerusalem to the cistern of Malchiah, son of Hammelech, in the court of the prison to lift Jeremiah from incarceration.

En route, Ebed-Melech's creativity kicked in as he considered a potential difficulty. If Jeremiah had sunk into the mud, a significant amount of force could be needed to extract him. It is possible that Jeremiah's sides and underarms could be injured by the coarseness of the ropes let down to lift him up. This "servant of God," desiring to do no harm to the manifested Word of God, altered his route and stopped by the king's house to search through the Royal

Goodwill storage, where all the worn and unwearable royal garments were stored. From these, he selected the most plush, thickest garments he could find and brought these tatters with him to the cistern.

Upon arrival, he spoke to the prophet not by name nor by title. Yet, his very presence spoke volumes. He instructed Jeremiah to wrap himself in the garments and cloths and place them between his flesh and the ropes as a cushion to prevent any bruising or scarring to his body.

The prophet listened, and without response, cushioned himself and obeyed the servant's instructions. He was then lifted from the cistern without bodily harm. It is in this instance, perhaps more than any other, that Ebed-Melech demonstrated what he learned on the down-low with Yahweh.

He learned how precious the Word of God is, and those of us who dare to lift it up, preach, and teach its statutes must do so with an attribute of power, tempered by compassion.

9

It's the Lord's blessings...we now enjoy.
—Traditional

What do we Believers know about "blessings"? Two major points come to mind: 1) God has an infinite number of blessings that never run out, and 2) once blessed, one cannot be cursed.

The first point is most dramatically illustrated in the story of Jacob and Esau, where Esau, the firstborn, sold his birthright to his brother for a bowl of lentil soup. In addition, this trickster Jacob and his mother Rebekah plotted to ensure that Jacob received Isaac's pronouncement of the patriarchal blessing. Isaac, blind in both eyes, bestowed the greater blessing on Jacob. When Esau approached his father later to receive the pronouncement, the deception was revealed as Isaac acknowledged that he has already declared his blessing on Esau, and it was not reversible.

Isaac declared, "I blessed him, and he shall be blessed!"

In Genesis 27:38, Jacob screamed, and asked, "Do you only have one blessing Father, is there no blessing for me?"

The second illustration regarding the nature of "blessings," is found in the Balaam and Balak story. Balak, one of the kings of Moab, intimidated by Israel's sprawling population, hires Balaam, a non-Israelite prophet to curse the

Children of Israel. After building several altars, several burnt offerings, and a few encounters with Yahweh, Balaam is forced to admit that he cannot curse what Yahweh has already blessed. It is with this backdrop that we approach Yahweh's blessing upon Ebed-Melech.

> Now the word of the Lord came unto Jeremiah, while he was shut up in the court of the prison, saying, Go and speak to Ebed-Melech the Ethiopian, saying, Thus saith the Lord of Host, The God of Israel: Behold, I will bring my words upon this city for evil and not for good; and they shall be accomplished in that day before thee. But I will deliver thee in that day, saith the Lord: and thou shalt not be given into the hand of the men of who thou art afraid. For I will surely deliver thee, and thou shall not fall by the sword, but thy life shall be for a prey unto thee: because thou has put thy trust in me, saith the Lord. (Jeremiah 39: 15-18)

Sometime after his rescue from the cistern, while still in the court of the prison, Jeremiah received an oracle from Yahweh – a word from the Lord.

This word came in the same prophetic formula as the many prophecies that Jeremiah had already delivered, "Thus saith the Lord of Hosts, the God of Israel."

Yet, it was preceded by instructions to deliver this word to the sole personage of Ebed-Melech, the Ethiopian.

Yahweh said, "Tell Ebed-Melech that my plans for Judah have not changed. Jerusalem will be destroyed by the Babylonians and the Temple will be burned to the ground. Its protective walls will be completely torn down. Further, let him know that he will see the fulfillment of these words with his own eyes. But I, the Lord, make two commitments to him: First, though he will be a witness to great devastation and deconstruction, I will deliver him when this occurs. Second, he will not be turned over to the men who he fears."

Jeremiah was further instructed by Yahweh to tell Ebed-Melech that he will be saved in the midst of all the death and dying that he will witness. *That, I, the Lord, will ensure that he will not be pierced by a sword, but that his life will be preserved for him as a 'prize.'*

The profoundness of this blessing compels closer analysis. One is immediately taken aback by the fact that Yahweh spoke to a eunuch at all. Deuteronomy 23:1 is direct in stating that a male whose testicles are crushed or whose penis has been detached from his body is forbidden to enter into the assembly of the Lord. This idea of being forbidden to stand in the presence of Yahweh implied a certain distancing from the presence and purview of Yahweh, even as it carried a connotation of shame within the community, particularly among people with strict societal gender roles.

Several theologians suggest that this chapter in Deuteronomy sought to identify membership in the Israelite community by inclusion and exclusion. Exclusion is linked to the ancient belief that sexual potency was a sign of divine blessing and wholeness. However, it is no small matter to note that without ecclesiastical standing, Yahweh spoke to Ebed-Melech.

To ensure that there is no confusion regarding the source of this oracle, Yahweh announced God's self with two Theo-historical identifiers: the Lord of Hosts and the God of Israel. It was well established that in ancient Near East culture, a name was not just a name or a label, but rather it implied character, identity, and existence. A name signified the nature of an individual.

Even as Jacob signified trickster, so it was with the Creator, informing us of the godly nature. The name The Lord, or Yahweh, occurred nearly 7000 times in the biblical texts, and was the most common designation for God in the

Hebrew Scriptures. Its etymology can be traced to Exodus 3:14 as a divine response to Moses, who suggested that the Israelites might well want to know the name of the God who was authorizing Moses' leadership and the projected liberation of children of Israel.

The response is, *"eheyeh asher eheyeh,"* "I am who I am" or "I will be who I will be." This is the name of the God of Israel. While certainly cryptic, and perhaps with intention, the response was appropriate for a god suggesting the divine enigmatic, mysterious, inexplicable, unknowable, and completely "other."

However, implicit in this definition are two additional inferences of significance. The first is the idea of a promise of divine presence, God will be present. To invoke the name "the God of Israel" brings to mind not only the call of Moses, but also the deliverance of Israel from Egyptian bondage. So, "I am who I am" was not just present, this God was active in the history of God's people.

The second inference is causative. Yahweh caused things to be brought into being and created. The name "Lord of Hosts" in Hebrew is *YHWH tseva 'oth*, a title that occurs more than 250 times in the biblical texts, along with a number of variations. In the Septuagint, it is rendered *Kyrios pantokrater*. This title is not found in the Pentateuch, nor in Joshua or Judges. It first appeared in the Hebrew Scriptures in connection with the sanctuary at Shiloh in I Samuel 4:4. Further, the title is used in association with the ark, which represented the enthroned presence of God. The concept of Yahweh as "enthroned king" brings to mind the Canaanite envisioning of their god, El.

It has been suggested that the original title of the deity was *el tseva'oath* (God of Host), with Hosts referring to the celestial beings and luminaries of the heavens that represent the armies that accompanied the Divine Warrior in I Samuel 17:45. These celestial beings also included those beings that were in attendance at the Divine Council.

Beyond the Divine's self-identification, the verses of this blessing contain four verbs that also demand our attention. The first three were actions that Yahweh promised to exercise in his protection of Ebed-Melech. The fourth was an emotive action employed by Ebed-Melech toward Yahweh, which inherently possessed its own rewards. This will be addressed separately.

Yahweh said, "I will deliver thee in that day....I will surely deliver thee, because thou has put thy trust in me."

The first deliverance verbs are *nathan* and *natsal*. The verb, *nathan*, is a common verb appearing more than 2000 times in the biblical texts, with a preponderance of being interpreted as "give," but it is translated as "to hand over" or "deliver" in about 180 instances. Theologically speaking, *nathan* is found in those contexts where God is said to have delivered his people from their enemies. So, in this sense, *nathan* is synonymous with *natsal*.

The verb *natsal* means deliverance from one's human enemies. This same verb describes Reuben's rescue of Joseph from his brothers in Genesis 37:21. In the book of Jeremiah, we see the verb used as a demand for justice in Jeremiah 21:12 and 22:3, where the Word of the Lord comes to Jeremiah calling for the deliverance of the oppressed in Israel. Its most common usage is the emphasis on Yahweh delivering his people from their enemies, as in Deuteronomy 23:14, Judges 8:34, I Samuel 12:10, and II Kings 18:30. We see the same verb also used in God's deliverance of Israel from the Egyptians in Exodus 2:19, 3:8, and 6:5; Judges 6:9; and Jeremiah 15:21. Additionally, it is used where Yahweh promised to deliver Jerusalem from those nations which held her captive, taking her into exile. A significant inference is that *nasal* is also used to describe the deliverance of Israel from her false prophets and unjust rulers, in Ezekiel 13:23 and 34:10.

A third verb for our consideration is *malat*. This verb appears about 90 times and carries the predominant sense of "escape." In a third of its usage and in varying contexts, it is translated as "deliver." There are a number of references where the verb refers to Yahweh delivering his people, as in Psalms 22:5 and 107:20. While other texts refer to a Divine promise to rescue or deliver Israel, as shown in Isaiah 46:4, Daniel 12:1, and Joel 2:32. There are also promises of the deliverance of Jerusalem, Jeremiah 39:18. Additionally, *malat* has a number of meanings related to the idea of flight or escape and the distinction between escape and flight is not precise.

Now, let us consider the fourth emotive verb *b-t-h*, "to trust."

Walter Brueggemann, noted Jeremiah scholar and authority, commented on Yahweh's salvific act toward Ebed-Melech by contrasting his "trust" in Yahweh over and against Jeremiah's admonishments to Judah not to trust in the claims regarding the Temple, Jeremiah 7:4. Brueggemann reasons that Judah had misplaced his trust and, as a result, experienced destruction. Ebed-Melech, an exception, performed a concrete act of trust by intervening on Jeremiah's behalf. Trust, however, was the end product of an assurance, and a proven ability to rely on the character, capacity, strength, and/or truth of someone – in this case Yahweh. The establishment of "trust" implies both a process, and inherently, an element of time.

The Hebrew verb for trust is *b-t-ch*, or *batach*. Its definition is most interesting, for while the derivatives of *b-t-h* reflect feelings of security - being unconcerned regarding reliability, the verb inherently carries a negative connotation. This connotation implies that which is relied upon may very well turn out to be deceptive. Many of the words derived from *b-t-ch* are used to convey a false security. Yet, at the same time, the words are used to convey the idea of complete security in God alone.

In the Septuagint, *b-t-ch* is interpreted in the negative sense by the word, *pepoithenai*, which shows up frequently in the books of Isaiah and Jeremiah, referring to false security. When one considers the passages in which *b-t-h* is used, the verb points to many things on which man can rely, yet in other instances can bring him to failure, as in Proverbs 11:28, Psalms 49:7 and 52:7, and Job 39:11. The exception to the rule is trust in Yahweh. Yahweh can be utterly relied upon and will not fail. Here, the LXX uses the word *elpizein*, which means "to hope."

Yahweh concluded his blessings to Ebed-Melech by acknowledging the servants unfailing trust, a trust that in and of itself produced certain blessings.

> Jeremiah 17:7-8 says, *Blessed is the man that trusteth in the Lord, and whose hope the Lord is. For he shall be as a tree planted by the waters, and that spreadeth out her roots by the river, and shall not see when heat cometh, but her leaf shall be green: and shall not be careful in the year of drought, neither shall cease from yielding fruit.*

So, in light of these expositions of appellations and verbs, let us turn again to Yahweh's blessing to Ebed-Melech:

> While Jeremiah was shut up in the court of the prison, the Word of the Lord came to him saying, "Go and speak to Ebed-Melech the Ethiopian. Tell him that I, the Lord, Yahweh; the I am who I am and the one who will be whom I will be; the I am God who is causative in my nature, and brings things into being, by my presence; I and all the celestial hosts and luminaries of the heavens, along with the hosts of the divine beings that attend the divine

council; I, the Lord of hosts, have some information that I want to pass along to you, concerning the political status of Judah and some personal information relating to Ebed-Melech. But before I inform you of that, so that there is not confusion regarding the source of this information, or the voice that you are hearing, know that I am the God of Israel; the one who rules all of nature and has the capacity to scatter my enemies by the outstretching of my hand. Now, as to what is about to occur: Jerusalem is about to be destroyed, including its Temple and its walls. Both shall be burned to the ground, and neither shall remain standing. But, in the midst of this destruction, pestilence, and strife, I am going to rescue you, Ebed-Melech, from those whom you fear and from those who are your enemies. Know that because I have spoken this word of deliverance, your enemies are my enemies. Therefore, in every threatening situation that you encounter, I will provide a means of escape. I will even deliver you from false prophets and false understandings. No weapon utilized against you will prove effective, and you will not fall by sword. But your life will be preserved as a prize to you. I am doing this because you put your trust in me. And, as a result of our trusting relationship, from this day forward your life will be fill with goodness. All that you need to flourish will be readily provided to you. Periods of scarcity will not hinder this promise to you, so when encountering scarcity, give it no thought. For you will forevermore experience a fruitful and productive life. (Jeremiah 39:15-18)

Given this understanding of Yahweh's blessing upon the Queer, how might we Queer Folx respond? I propose we consider the following:

Seven Major Attributes of Black Queer Inspired Leadership

Self-Love and Self-Knowledge

In Toni Morrison's novel, *Beloved*, she has the matriarch, Baby Suggs, preach a succinct yet profound sermon. Baby Suggs says:

> *Here…in this place, we flesh: flesh that weeps, laughs; flesh that dances on bare feet in grass. Love it. Love it hard. Yonder [pointing to the other side of the Ohio River where slavery is legal] they do not love your flesh. They despise it. They don't love your eyes; they'd just as soon pick 'em out. No more do they love the skin on your back. Yonder they flay it. And O my people they do not love your hands. Those they only use, tie, bind, chop off and leave empty. Love your hands! Love them. Raise them up and kiss them. Touch others with them…stroke them on your face 'cause they don't love that either. You got to love it, you!*

Abdul R. JanMohamed in "Negating the Negation as a Form of Affirmation in Minority Discourse" provides us with some understanding of the necessity of this prerequisite process of self-love as he plumbs the depths of Richard Wright's auto-biography, *Black Boy*, to expose the societal forces of Jim Crow; enforceable laws and behaviors relegating African Americans to subaltern positions of existence, post-emancipation.

These codes and traditions of southern hegemony seek to position Black men (and women) somewhere between "social death" and suicide. Albert

Memmi in *The Colonizer and the Colonized*, offers a similar analysis suggesting that these daily operative forces are purposefully designed to limit Black maturation to that of "a sub-human creature devoid of initiative and entirely compliant to the will of white supremacy."

Memmi suggests that the very hegemonic formation of minorities is based on an attempt to negate them. Further, the larger goal of the project is to prevent minorities (i.e. "others") from realizing their potential as human beings, as well as preventing their full and equal participation in the larger civil and political society.

The author's prevailing conclusion is that minorities cannot take part in, or provide, effective leadership in the dominant society of which they are members, until there has been an individual and personal negation of these negative hegemonic forces. If one is Black and Queer, the game is called "Double Dutch."

From a philosophical perspective, self-knowledge may be understood as knowledge of one's unique and particular mental state. This knowledge is inclusive of one's beliefs, desires, and sensations. It is also referred to as knowledge regarding one's persisting self – its ontological nature and character traits. Self-knowledge is distinctive, in that we come to it through a methodology of careful introspection, guided by our unique positions to regulate our own mental states. Additionally, our pronouncements regarding our own states bear a special authority or presumption of truth.

Discernment

The act of discernment is related to issues of wisdom, combined with some degree of objectivity. It is a primary characteristic in elements of religious and spiritual development, and can be understood as the ability to judge wisely and critically. The early church father St. Ignatius believed that the primary relationship between the Believer and the Divine was established in the heart or the interior dimension of the individual. For St. Ignatius, every human being is called to a specific and general vocation. The general vocation of all humans is to revere, praise, and serve God. St. Ignatius believed that when the "Call of God" was communicated to heart, the results are a stirring of the emotions and the identifying of those emotions by the intellect points to the will of God for the individual.

Also, contributing to the need for discernment is the recognition that all creation is permeated by both goodness and evil. Here, evil may be understood as both the consequence of sin and a personal force. It is the desire of the Believer to respond to the word and the purposes of the Christ – to do good and not evil. Therefore, it is the task of the Believer to discern the movement of the Spirit in the time and circumstances of their lived experience – to see clearly, even in times of darkness. Discernment permeates the narrative of Ebed-Melech.

Agency

Agency may be simplistically defined as the faculty of acting or working as a means to an end. However, when viewed psychologically, human agency has four central properties: intentionality, forethought, self-reactiveness, and self-reflectiveness.

Individuals create and engage in the development of plans and strategies they believe can influence and shape their preferred future. Further, people regulate their thinking; thinking ahead of time, determining and anticipating likely outcomes of their actions.

Self-reactiveness is where the individual not only makes plans and related ideas, but also constructs appropriate courses of action and monitors their execution.

The final property of human agency is self-reflectiveness. Through proactive self-awareness (self-knowledge), humans can reflect on the soundness of their thinking, the strength of their capacities, and the meaning of their pursuits. Through this process of reflection, corrections and adjustments, plans, actions, strategies, and goals are created.

In addition to these core properties, agency operates in three modes: individual, proxy, and collective. Individual agency is when a person brings personal influence to bear on lived circumstance. If the individual does not have the capacity to accomplish this end, he or she may well appeal to someone else who can. Children turn to parents, students turn to teachers, and so forth. Lastly, certain instances require people to work together toward a desired outcome or in a collective manner. The Ebed-Melech narrative exemplifies all three of these modes.

Creativity

To be creative is to be inventive, imaginative, and original, and to exhibit imagination, as well as intellect. Creativity is not just originality, but must also have some sort of value and/or solve a problem. And yet, creativity is not just problem solving, but also includes problem finding. Problem finding is related to the identification of a problem which previously was unseen. In fact, many creative people believe problem identification is more important to creative achievement than problem solving. Creativity can also be understood as self-expression, as in artistic performances. Creativity as a personality trait is tied to motivation, yet does not simply emerge. Creativity appears to be a trait that people work at, study, and intentionally nurture. This trait is linked to the intrinsic interest that appears to provide increased capacities for considering numerous options and finding original insight.

The Swiss psychiatrist, Carl Jung (1875 – 1961), theorized that another characteristic that may contribute to creativity is the capacity to tap into the unconscious. Jung's view of creativity and the unconscious appears to be consistent with the idea of incubation and its role, creatively. Many famous creators suggest that good ideas and insights depend on this kind of incubation and surface as "aha moments." Ebed-Melech displayed great creativity in his arguments to King Zedekiah to remove Jeremiah from the cistern in the rescue strategy, and even moreso in choosing to cushion Jeremiah from any potential harm from rope burn.

Liminality

In her dissertation, "The Hidden Eunuch of the Hebrew Bible: Uncovering an Alternate Gender," Janet S. Everhart discusses the definition and function of liminality. Everhart defines liminality as the eunuch's ability to cross varied thresholds that are barriers to cis (hetero-normative) men and women. Everhart views this capacity as a source of the eunuch's power.

Though often on the margins of society, eunuchs can literally be found guarding various thresholds. Eunuchs move between the world of the king and his women, facilitating communication and often carrying messages from one powerful person to another. They acquire access to the most intimate functions in the lives of powerful men and women, such as bathing the women and guarding the kings as they sleep.

While Ebed-Melech's specific responsibilities are not outlined in the rescue narrative, his access and liminality are prominent; he can leave his assigned post at will, approach the king without summons or introduction, and appears to have "carte blanche" to the kingdom's resources. In the same manner that colonialism and the colonized mind are precursors to institutional racism, liminality is the precursor to multi-culturalism. Liminality suggests a capacity and appreciation for the positive engagement of varied peoples, ideologies, expressions, and communities.

Power Tempered by Compassion

This culminating leadership attribute may well be more an outcome of acquired equipoise, resulting from the synergy of the preceding six characteristics, than an individual trait. Without question, Ebed-Melech is a powerful individual, deriving power from each of the qualities we have described. Yet, permeating his persona is a strong sense of compassion that appears to influence how he uses his power.

The Oxford Dictionary indicates that the original source of the word "compassion" is Old French (prior to 1400 C.E.), taken from ecclesiastical Latin (*compassion* (n), from *compati*), meaning to suffer with. The modern definition is to have sympathetic pity and concern for the suffering or misfortune of others.

When Ebed-Melech stops off at the Royal Goodwill to find some plushy garments to protect Jeremiah, his behavior is telling. First, his actions say this is not his first rodeo! He has been here before. He knows the potential costs of the extraction process. Secondly, through discernment and agency, he demonstrates just how precious he views Jeremiah, the manifested Word of God. We might be a little careful as we consider this encounter. Does it not provide us an opportunity to redefine and reconcile the relationship between Queer people and the Word of God? To be a two-way relationship, those who believe they represent the Word of God might also need to redefine and reconcile.

10

There's a man over the river...givin' sight to the blind.
—Traditional

But He said to them, "All cannot accept this saying, but only those to whom it has been given: For there are eunuchs who were born thus from their mother's womb, and there are eunuchs who were made eunuchs by men, and there are eunuchs who have made themselves eunuchs for the kingdom of heaven's sake. He who is able to accept it, let him accept it. (Matthew 19:11-12)

In the latter part of the decade of the 1950's, Momma became an entrepreneur. She bought the beauty shop she had been working in from Aunt Sweetie when Sweetie finished her bachelor's degree and became a public school teacher. I learned of this change the day they replaced the two large plate glass windows in the front of the building, changing the name of the business to "Berdine's Beauty Parlor." The building was on Church Street, a major artery of Norfolk, Virginia that ran through the heart of the ghetto into the downtown business district. Next door, was Mr. Payne's grocery store, a Jewish man who ran the business with his wife. But across the street, the Harold family opened up their own grocery store.

The Harold's were a Black family who lived on the outskirts of the city, in what was called "the rural." Their store had a larger variety of products; fresh produce and even fresh meats. Momma would on occasion buy a case of chickens from the Harold's. It would be my job to de-ice them and place them in plastic bags. She would always send a couple of chickens to her poorest clients with children. We also bought our milk and other major purchases from Harold's, but I still patronized Mr. Payne's because he had two-for-a-nickel cookies and candies.

On almost any given day, along the shaded side wall of Harold's market, the "community drunks" would congregate. They would jokingly harass me from time to time as I made my way into Harold's.

One would yell out, "Hey there young fellow...give me a quarter."

I would answer back, "I ain't got no quarter!"

He would retort, "Ain't you something...You are the original man...Black and broke, and don't know who you are...Have a good day!"

On another day, one of his fellow drunks might say, "Hey, church boy...give me 50 cents."

I would say, "I ain't got 50 cents."

He would say, "You still praying to that white Jesus?"

I would answer, "Yes."

His retort, "I'm praying for you, that your knowledge might increase!"

And their fellowship would break out into laughter.

A quarter of a century would pass before Lucy, a 3.2-million-year-old fossil skeleton would be discovered in Hadar, Ethiopia. A half-century would pass before I would witness two popes kneel and pray before a Russian iconograph of the Black Madonna and her son, the Black Jesus, the Christ. Subjugated Truth!

Michel Foucault, a French philosopher of the 1960s through the 1980s, who was the first public figure in France to die of HIV, provides tremendous insight for us in this area of thought. He seems to imply that subjugated Truth is a necessity for the maintenance of a society's dominant narrative. Foucault suggests that knowledge is power; that knowledge and power are one; and that knowledge, oppression, power, and truth hold enormous implications for the lived experience of marginalized communities.

The privileging of the methods of science, and what Foucault calls "Unitary Knowledge," has led to the subjugation and erasure of previously established erudite knowledge, including local, popular, and indigenous - predominately located at the margins of society. These indigenous knowledges have been exiled from the legitimate domain of formal knowledge. Foucault argues that the countering and correctives to these privileged knowledges has not come through counter-argument nor debate, but rather through what he terms, "the insurrection of subjugated knowledge:" The Women's Movement, Civil Rights Movement, Womanist Movement, Stonewall, and I would add, the Fellowship of Affirming Ministries and their mission of de-pathologizing Black Queer Believers.

As we move toward our summation and the preliminary Theological implications of the Ebed-Melech narrative, let us consider a brief word regarding the Black hermeneutic.

The Black hermeneutic encompasses the theories and methods of biblical interpretation employed by enslaved Africans and expanded upon by the succeeding generations of Black preachers and scholars. Its communal purpose is to extract meaning that speaks to the social location, lived reality, and resulting consciousness of African American Christian Believers. At a more profound level, it seeks to decenter Western hegemonic biblical interpretation that has historically supported racism, enslavement, segregation, colonialism, capitalism, patriarchy and anti-wokeness. As such, the Black hermeneutic views the central reality of the biblical text as liberative, in contrast to domination. The

Black hermeneutic may have emerged initially from the intuitiveness of Black preachers, both male and female, who "sat where they, enslaved Africans, sat."

It is clear that these biblical pioneers did not exegete the text with the intellectual formality of our day. However, they did seek the guidance of the Holy Spirit and Its resurrection power that they might speak in the same words of Jeremiah, "The Word of the Lord came unto me saying..."

To this end, the Black hermeneutic can be identified historically in the earliest recorded African American sermons.

Frank A. Thomas, in his book, *They Like to Never Quit Praisin' God*, records the genius of the African American preaching tradition by referencing a sermon entitled "Uncle Walsh's Funeral." Recorded in an enslaved narrative authored in 1936, Ned Walker heard the sermon around 1866-67. Uncle Walsh was the blacksmith in his community, locating his business in the fork of the road across from a major church. He had been a very strong man and had used his trade on behalf of all the people of his community. Walsh had joined the Spring Valley African Methodist Episcopal Church, but had fallen from grace. He had been accused of stealing master Walter Bryce's pig, and there was evidence suggesting his guilt. Walsh was sent to prison, and while there, he contracted consumption and died.

Uncle Pompey preached the funeral. Pompey was noted for his ability to preach a powerful funeral.

The central question in the minds of Black people was, "If you go to jail, can you also go to heaven?"

Pompey took his text from the story of Paul and Silas locked in jail. He began by talking about Uncle Walsh, his life of hard work and bravery. Uncle Walsh tackled kicking horses and mules, so that the crops could be cultivated and harvested and the community fed. Pompey suggested that it wasn't eternally against the church member to have gone to prison, for the text states that Paul and Silas were locked in jail, and he was certain that they made it into heaven.

Pompey then began to talk about a vision of Jacob's ladder, envisioning Uncle Walsh as he climbed Jacob's ladder into heaven. He concluded his sermon by having the congregation sing "There is a Fountain Filled with Blood."

As they began to sing the second verse about the dying thief, Pompey cried out above the crowd, "I see brother Walsh as he enters in, and that dying thief is there to welcome him, thank God!"

With that declaration, those assembled broke into great celebration and shouting. Clearly, the Black hermeneutic was all over Pompey's sermon.

The Black hermeneutic also has roots in the sociological analysis of W.E.B. Du Bois, describing the consciousness of the American Negro when he wrote, "The Negro is a sort of seventh son, born with a veil, and gifted with a second-sight in this American world – a world that yields him no true self-consciousness, but only lets him see himself through the revelation of the other world."

Du Bois concludes that this unique sociopolitical positioning of the Black community produces a double consciousness. People of African descent living in the United States must come to psychologically function within both the dominant culture and their own unique subculture. The Black hermeneutic emerges from this survival technique.

Henry H. Mitchell introduces the Black hermeneutic to academia by reminding us of the distinctive nature of the Black religious experience in America. He insists that this experience was given a religious interpretation by those who were innocent of the white exegetical biblical tradition. Their interpretations emerged from their African consciousness and correspondence with the Bible. They preached as best they could, seeking a greater understanding of the biblical texts as they also sought to make sense of their lived experience.

Mitchell argues that the best of Black preaching is basically unchanged from the methodologies employed by the earliest Black preachers because "Black preaching...was not in the mainstream of the changing world of white theology."

For Mitchell, the two main principles of the Black hermeneutic are: 1) the gospel is declared in the vernacular of the people, and 2) the gospel speaks directly to the contemporary man/woman and their needs.

A third component of the Black hermeneutic and Black biblical studies is the exploration and identification of the Black presence in the biblical text. For people of African descent, this approach provides a multilevel connectedness with biblical stories, an intense sociopolitical connection, and a direct racial connection. The identification of a historical presence of Black people in the Bible began in the nineteenth century with Black preachers, such as J.W.C Pennington and Henry Highland Garnett, and continues into the twentieth century with such scholars as Charles Copher, Renita Weems, Delores Williams and Cain Hope Felder.

Through a variety of academic approaches, these scholars have identified a strong Black presence in the Bible. Beyond their initial focus on discrete Black individuals, such as Hagar or Zipporah, Moses's Cushite wife, or Ebed-Melech, subsequent scholarship has progressed to demonstrate that the context and culture of the biblical world were located on the continent of Africa and were significantly influenced by an African consciousness. Therefore, the primary assertion of Black biblical hermeneutics in the current century is not only that there are Black people in the Bible, but also that the corpus itself is set in an African context, both geographically and culturally. In this writing, I have titled these overt instances of Black parallelism as "Black Tendencies." Among the most profound of these parallels is the sociopolitical parallel found in the book of Jeremiah, the Hananiah/Jeremiah debate found in the 28th Chapter.

In the same year that Nebuchadnezzar plundered Jerusalem, taking the golden vessels of worship along with 10,000 Judahites back to Babylon, he also set up Zedekiah as king. Hananiah, another prophet of equal status with Jeremiah, prophesied in a public setting before the priest and the people that all of the damage done by Nebuchadnezzar would be reversed in a span of two years. Hananiah expresses the sentiment of a true nationalist. He believed that God would not destroy Judah, but would restore the nation, in direct contradiction to the prophecies of Jeremiah.

Jeremiah's advice to Judahites was to accept their conquered status, go into exile, and assimilate; build houses and vineyards and procreate - integrate. These two biblical prophets and their differing approaches in the face of oppression parallel the sociopolitical visions of two of the greatest African American prophets, Dr. Martin Luther King, Jr. and el-Hajj Malik el-Shabazz (Malcolm X).

Furthering this proposition of Black tendencies in the book of Jeremiah, we turn now to the Theological wrestlings of the Ebed-Melech narrative with this caveat. In his introduction to *The Original African Heritage Study Bible*, Cain Hope Felder seeks to correct what he calls "the misconception." This misconception is the view that almost all biblical characters are Caucasian. Felder argues that the Bible is multiracial and multicultural, with a divine purpose as a universal story of salvation. It is my hope that my Queer Caucasian brothers and sisters will transcend the conforming forces of "whiteness," and embrace the universal salvific principles of the Ebed-Melech narrative.

Of Ebed-Melech

I find theological significance in our inclusive representation in this narrative. That the Creator, in Her brilliance, recorded for posterity a narrative celebrating in one character, the giftedness of the intersectionality of Blackness and Queerness. Inclusion brings with it its own rewards. Our inclusion as Black Queer men in this text affirms our Divine acceptance. We are not an anathema. We are not an abomination. We are a unique and highly favored creation of unshackled, gifted imagination and unlimited creativity. Not hated because we are weak, hated because we refuse to bow to the prescribed images of the Du Bois mirror; seeing ourselves as others see us. No, we are called to self-define. And we see ourselves, as all human beings, gifted with breath, creations of the Most High God. Even though our existence pushes against the limiting imaginary of white male patriarchy.

Our inclusion in the biblical text is a beginning place for those who choose to minister to us. Celebrate with us our inclusion. Preach it to us and raise our self-esteem. Tell of it far and wide, mitigating our loneliness, anxiety, and depression. We must come to view our intersectionality as a lens. Not just seeing the multiple layers of oppression, such as racism, homophobia, and classism that we face, but rather, seeing, excavating, and highlighting the indigenous knowledges which have nurtured our survival.

When I reflect on discovering the Ebed-Melech narrative as a focus of study, I am reminded of the late Reverend James Moore, gospel recording artist for Malaco Records. Moore recorded a song entitled, "He Was There All the Time:"

He was there all the time
He was there all the time
Waiting patiently in light
He was there all the time

The beauty of the Ebed-Melech narrative is that it is not creative fiction of the Black imaginary, rather it is a biblically-based, salvific narrative.

The name Ebed-Melech is the consequence of the collision of two divergent Hebrew words; Ebed, the word for servant, and Melech, the word for king. The barer of this name brings into light a prism of "embodied energies" on a continuum which stretches from the wisdom of a servant to the authority of a king. Servant wisdom, similar to that displayed by Naaman's servants who soothed his ego and coaxed him into dipping seven times in the muddy Jordan river. An act facilitating his healing from leprosy in II Kings 5:1-27.

At the other end of this continuum is the authority of a king. Here, I suggest that we consider the knowledges of authority displayed by the Centurian whose servant was ill at his home. Jesus offers to go to the soldier's home, but the man rejects that idea, saying he is not worthy that Jesus should enter into his dwelling. In his rebuttal, the Centurian articulates his knowledges regarding authority. He explains that he serves under authority and there are other men who are under his authority. He describes the command/obedience, authority/power model, after which he makes an assessment of Jesus' authority/power and draws his conclusion.

He concludes that Jesus' authority appears to be related to the authority/power model of kings. Maybe, even the King of Kings. After making an assessment of the capacities of Jesus, he concludes that Jesus has sufficient power and authority to heal and deliver his servant right where Jesus was standing. He perceives that it is not necessary for Jesus to take another step. Neither, does He need to face the direction of his dwelling. The Centurian concludes that all Jesus has to do, is "to speak the word, only," in Matthew 8:8-13.

So, the name Ebed-Melech suggests a continuum of qualities and giftings ranging from the wisdom of servants to the authority of kingship. Given the breadth of this continuum, there is a position for every Black male impacted by the sociopolitical knowledges of this current era. To this end, Ebed-Melech is a metaphor for the African American males living in the United States of

America in the 21st century, gay or straight. And, as if this challenge to become an informed and impactful leader were not enough, Ebed-Melech beckons us to achieve this goal with Black Excellence.

We should not be deceived, Ebed-Melech's rescue of the prophet Jeremiah is, by far, the greatest achievement of his life. This single act far outstrips all of the service he has provided to the king and the kingdom. This single act settles any question of purpose that may have ever plagued his mind. Bringing with its completion, a sense of wholeness, and an added touch of unspeakable joy.

He exudes and exemplifies for Black males the internal work of negating the societal negations, in turn negating the Du Bois mirror. An act that aspiring Black males must achieve to become grounded in the power of self-love and self-knowledge; a power that is an essential prerequisite to any form of leadership. He calls us to employ discernment prior to initiating any agency, reminding us of the power of our creative juices, which most often have been our saving grace. He challenges us to pursue a wisdom and the skill of liminality, allowing us to cross many thresholds, always being welcomed to return. Ebed-Melech is a metaphor for all Black males.

Missing from this narrative is Jeremiah's perspective on this incident. What we do know, however, is that up to the day he was thrown into the cistern, he had prophesied to Judah for 40 years, concluding with the kingship of Zedekiah in 586 B.C.E. Forty years of faithfully delivering the Word of God. Now, to find himself sealed in a perverted grave could not have felt like a just reward for his unwavering faithfulness to Yahweh. He had already been arrested on more than one occasion and had been severely beaten for his pronouncements, yet, he was faithful. But now, as the prophecies come to pass, he finds himself sequestered in a grave; a cavity whose purpose has been perverted.

Israel suffered long seasons of dryness and it had very few natural springs.

Its life preserving solution was to dig into the earth or carve into rock, creating an artificial reservoir for the collection and storing of water. The purpose of this cistern was to preserve life, not destroy it.

Yet, this is where Jeremiah finds himself, sealed off in utter darkness, and as Weldon Johnson writes…"as far as the eye of God could see…Darkness covered everything, blacker than a hundred midnights. Down in a cypress swamp."

Encased, after forty years of faithfulness, as all the major authorities are rushing to leave the desolation of the city, Jeremiah had to wonder, 'Is this how it ends?' Left to sink into the mud in utter darkness? To never see the light of day again? To contemplate at a deep level, 'Is this is what it means to die? Is this the time? Is this my place of death?'

Because the narrative does not share with us Jeremiah's perspective on his experience in the cistern, we don't know if he received prophetic utterances while in this death trap. Did Yahweh speak to him? I feel confident in asserting that Jeremiah did speak to him. Did Yahweh tell him that this was not his end? That this was not the place of his death? We do not know. But, I do know this, that when Ebed-Melech cracked the seal on that cistern, allowing the sunlight to break through the density of the darkness, and announced that he and 30 soldiers had come to save Jeremiah, from Jeremiah's perspective, Ebed-Melech took the sting out of death!

And, when he had instructed him to place the plush garments around and under his arms and threw down the ropes, lifting him out of the cistern, Ebed-Melech's agency took the victory from the grave. When Jeremiah had been fully rescued, and when the two men were able to come into full fellowship with each other, Jeremiah and Ebed-Melech witnessed and experienced a foretaste of resurrection power.

Ebed-Melech foreshadows the Christ as he is called to save the manifested word of God – Jeremiah. According to the scriptures, Christ came for the same purpose - to save, and then fulfill the Word of God.

> *Then said I, Lo, I come (in the volume of the book it is written of me,) to do thy will, O God.* (Hebrews 10:7)

Given Jesus' own definition, they are both eunuchs. Ebed-Melech, a eunuch made of men. Jesus, a eunuch for the sake of the kingdom.

Postlude

Fire keeps on burnin'...I can't hold my peace...
—Traditional
Pilate said to him, "What is truth?"
—John 18:38

Two similitudes immediately come to mind as we consider the relationship between the formative portion of my lived experience and the Theological reflections of the Ebed-Melech narrative. First, they are both rescue narratives. Rescue is a central theme of the Hebrew Scriptures, beginning with Noah and the boat to the "Children" walking across the "Reed Sea" on dry land. In fact, rescue is ubiquitous in the entirety of the biblical text. The prevailing promise of the Holy Writ is that Believers are rescued from the penalty of sin, death, hell and the grave by the salvific act of God in Christ Jesus. Believers are and will ultimately be, Saved!

The second similitude is a sub-text that outlines the journey toward the self. The Ebed-Melech narrative, considered at a deeper level, is a self-revelation of divine purpose. A Black male, survives physical, societal, and religious castrations, and then evolves to become the agent of rescue for the manifested Word of God. Without question, this single act was the greatest accomplishment of his life. The success of this one task required all of the skills he had ever attained; cognitive, political, and otherwise. Ebed-Melech was not the same man after the rescue of Jeremiah that he was when Yahweh first called him to the task. Yahweh's blessing was simply a bonus to the experience.

In the reality of our day-to-day existence, one is seldom certain as to how deliverance will emerge. Will rescue come from the agency of a known or an unknown entity? Will the Creator intervene in some unique manner we had not considered? Or, is this the instance in which we will need to rise up and deliver ourselves?

I write to the young, somewhere between their learning and earning years, who are Queer or who love a Queer individual. One may be fearful for them because of the derogatory pronouncements of the biblical illiterates who have passionately weaponized the Word against Queer humanity. I also write to these unlettered and "twisted" pastors - preachers, even as I write to the parents and family of Queer children to remind them that no one knows the vastness of the mind of God. Let me say this one more time: No one knows the vastness of the mind of God! At best, and even among the most sacred of us, we are all like Jacob, wrestling to define the full meaning of God's presence in our lives.

Our sociocultural prejudice toward Queerness is rooted in the confluence of whiteness, patriarchy with its spirit of dominance, and the restrictive limited literary imagination of many white biblical interpreters, both male and female. Traditional whiteness has only one membership criteria - white maleness. Given its dominating purpose, it demands the exclusion of all others. Whiteness, and its supporters, constitute the community which perpetrates this Theo-sociopolitical distortion of reality. And most interestingly, they would have us believe that this nation is trapped in a political force field that cannot be changed; stuck in a scenario that cannot be altered.

In a multi-cultural world, what impedes us? Perhaps it is because most whites are only fluent in one cultural expression, and that is whiteness. This intrinsic construct values no other culture as equal to their own. Whiteness does what it does, and would have us believe that it is always right, particularly as it relates to issues of power.

Nevertheless, this lack of cultural competence is a major chink in the would-be king's armor.

I also write to those of us gifted with intersectionality, the Black, Brown, Red, Yellow and Queer; those who have been disadvantaged by multiple layers of oppression, race, sexual preference, homophobia, and classism - Forces which often act together exacerbating the context. I write to remind these individuals that we have always existed. We have the power of presence. We are so ancient, as to be remembered in the biblical text and before. We are the uniquely created, Divinely inspired, twin and infinite spirits of creation; the sui generis of the species, gifted with a creative energy which permeates and undergirds our lived and current reality. It is this Divine gifting of an infinite imaginary, and the vast powers it yields, which forges the materiality of the well-spring of our indomitable spirit. In our full and activated selves – we are a tsunami.

As I write to you, our nation is experiencing a context of Theo-sociopolitical disruption. The most visceral appears to be the sociopolitical and the dystopian dominating narrative espoused by the oligarchs. The majority of the United States of America seems, by hook or by crook, to have elected a so-called president who seeks to be a "would-be-king." He seeks the regression of the entire nation to the old power model of sovereignty and obedience. He is employing a compressed campaign of "shock and awe." Simultaneously, blatant instances of criminality have come to light in the Supreme Court and the Congress. With undeniable corruption in all three branches of government being openly displayed, it brings into question the validity of the nation's construct of "law and order".

Perhaps this would not be so bad, in and of itself, if the religious institutions were in a more stable position. But they are not. Catholicism is busy settling sexual abuse cases, and making their confession regarding the subjugation of the Black Christ. On the other hand, the Methodists have split over the issue of Queerness. Newer church expressions and independent non-denominational churches are still reeling from the eisegetical whirlwinds of prosperity preaching. Not to mention that this same church body was instrumental in the overturning of Roe, and a return to the subjugation of women. A majority of white women continue to believe that their greatest security resides in the construct of whiteness, voting against their self-interest- even in the disturbing face of this most recent election.

The legacy media, our ultimate purveyor of whiteness, continuously peddles its daily reports with a high inference of normalcy, presenting disruptive societal positions cloaked in a magic garment which prevents legacy from acknowledging its ability to affect change. In addition to subjugating truths, particularly those truths in contradiction to the dominating narrative, it engages in coded language, distorting reality. For example, the last election was not about the high cost of groceries, or inflation. The election was about white domination/rule or symbolic Black governance; language that was never clearly articulated. A racial reality too stark to openly display in public, resulting in our first major presidential tyrant.

Legacy media seems to have some difficulty speaking to the visceral presence of racism in our society, despite its pervasiveness. The nature of reporting seems to be filtered through a sieve of discerning what's important for the masses to know. Legacy has a number of primary questions. Who and what do we elevate? What's our lead story? How does it support or negate the dominating narrative? For which group is the newest story potentially a major disruption? A redefining? What is our most benign response?

More recently we have witnessed the silencing of Black Voices.

The irrefutable truth is that there is no monopoly on what it means to be an American. And, there is no definition of American that does not include the humanity, contributions, and influence of African Americans. It is important for the marginalized to think beyond legacy media, to know our strength, and to know that our work is not done; to know that it is within our capacity and privilege to continue to shape the dominating narrative of the nation. In ways that the dominating culture does not even understand. Thank you, Kendrick Lamar!

We will prevail in this season, in part, because we have been here before. Our innate creativity moved us from an illiterate people to being predominantly literate in a 45-year period, from 1865 to 1910. The greatest educational transformation of any people – ever!

Since this transformation, the contributions of Black Excellence have emerged in every area of discipline. I submit that these accomplishments were significantly furthered by the formidable weapon of our religious experience.

Having observed the Black religious experience for some period of time, it becomes clear that the energizing force of *Jube*, Black religious celebration, is rooted in our sense of gratitude. Its essence permeates our prayers and ignites our praise. Its alchemy is an indigenous subjugated truth. Somewhere between the "Yes, Lord," the Pentecostal spiritual instructions of Charles Harrison Mason and the humility of Baptist deacons who postured themselves as "head bowed and body bent" as they approached God's throne of Grace, we as Believers have come to understand the transformative power of gratitude. To be thankful for what we have, be it little or much, and to recognize that whatever our state of being, Emanuel, God is with us. And God with us, is more than the world against us.

Lastly, it is important for all Queer people to know, we are blessed. That is the conclusion of the Ebed-Melech narrative. Yahweh says, "tell Ebed-Melech...

For I will surely deliver thee, and thou shalt not fall by the sword, but thy life shall be for a prize unto thee: because thou has put thy trust in me, saith the Lord." We are a blessed people!

As a pastor, there is always the question as to whether or not the message of our ministry is impactful. When I pastored in Maryland, there was a woman-led family with two teenage boys, both clearly gifted young men. After a few months, I began to notice that they would recite the benediction with me at the close of the service. I give it to you now...

As the Angel of the Lord, assigned to Queer People throughout the
world,
I bless you in Jesus' name.
I bless your coming in and your going out,
Your lying down and your rising up
I bless the labor of your hand and the fruit of that labor,
I bless the very creativity of your mind,
That it shall yield you the prosperity to which God has purposed you.
I speak health to your body,
That you will prosper in health, even as your soul prospers,
And I speak a word of peace,
That the Peace of God that passeth all understanding,
will set up residence in your life, tabernacle with you,
Now and forever more.
And the people of God say, Amen! Amen! Amen!

About the Author

Dr. Arthur Leon Tredwell was adopted at the age of four. His parent's belief in the "Narrative of Civility," the axiom that suggests if Black people live orderly lives and assimilate toward whiteness, then they can achieve the American Dream, assured that he would pursue higher education.

Dr. Tredwell is a graduate of Concordia College in Moorhead, Minnesota and majored in Political Science and Sociology. He earned his master's degree in Theology and Biblical Interpretation from United Theological Seminary in St. Paul, Minnesota. He then went on to obtain his Doctorate from the Joint Doctoral Program of the University of Denver and Iliff School of Theology, with an emphasis in Religion and Social Change. His research was focused on the intersection of race, class, gender, sexuality and the biblical text.

Dr. Tredwell has worked in several major business sectors including international grain trading for Cargill, the largest privately held corporation in the nation. In the government sector, he created an adoption program that dramatically increased adoptions of Black children in foster care in the state of Minnesota. In 2000, he founded a community development corporation and created 130 units of affordable housing.

For nine years, Reverend Tredwell pastored Christ Temple of Brooklyn Park, Minnesota, and provided spiritual guidance to over 100 Liberian and African American families. Additionally, he has served as senior pastor in Austin, Texas and in College Park, Maryland.